The Forever Fight

by

James M. Kilby

To: Agni,

Peace and Love

James M. Kilby

5-26-01

DORRANCE PUBLISHING CO., INC.
PITTSBURGH, PENNSYLVANIA 15222

Printed in the United States of America
ISBN 0-8059-4170-3

Second Printing

For information or to order additional books, please write:
Dorrance Publishing Co., Inc.
643 Smithfield Street
Pittsburgh, Pennsylvania 15222
U.S.A.
1-800-788-7654

Dedication

My wife: Mrs. Janice C. Kilby My children: Mrs. Racquelia Kilby Neal (daughter); Mr. Jamont Vidal Kilby (son); Mr. James W. Kilby (Father); Mrs. Catherine E. Kilby (mother) Grandchildren: Trevon Kilby-Neal, Corey Ian Neal, Nigel J. Kilby (grandsons); Mrs. Betty Kilby Fisher and Mrs. Patricia Kilby Robb (sisters); Mr. John F. Kilby and Mr. Gene M. Kilby (brothers); Mrs. Ester Kilby and Mrs. Michelle Kilby (sister-in-laws); Mr. Andrew Fisher and Mr. Nathaniel Robb (two brothers-in-law). To all my nieces, nephews, cousins and relatives. The nineteen Warren County original black students and their parents. Those community leaders, the community people and the Washington D.C. Educational Committee who supported the integration struggle in Front Royal, Virginia. These three attorneys, Oliver W. Hill, Otto Tucker and S.W. Tucker and my ghostwriter, Mr. Michael Brodie.
Peace and love to all mankind.

Contents

Introduction

Hell Town. That was what they used to call Front Royal, Virginia, when I was very young. A white gentleman was reminding us all of that history on May 7, 1996, as we celebrated the election of our town's first black mayor.

It had been thirty-five years since Frank Grier and I graduated from Front Royal's Warren County High School with our white classmates—the first blacks to do so. Today the school, the restaurants, the stores, and the movie theaters have all been integrated. We are no longer barred from the old Moose Lodge, as was the case when I was young. We can now try on our clothes at the store before we buy them. And now we can even run for public office—and win.

My sister, Betty, was the first black to run for the mayor's seat in 1990. With a predominantly black campaign staff, she managed slightly more than one-third of the votes. Two years before that she ran unsuccessfully for city council. George Banks and his nearly all-white inner circle secured a landslide victory, and so we celebrated.

Everybody was gathered in the American Legion Hall—the white one we were not allowed into once upon a time—our ears glued to the radio broadcast as the announcement came that Banks, a U.P.S. delivery man by day, was holding a sizable lead over Carson Lauder, a white former classmate of mine at Warren County High who now runs a local restaurant founded by his parents.

"Can you believe that Hell Town has elected a black mayor?" a man drunkenly asked Leon Thompson, a black friend of Banks who was a coworker from U.P.S. Leon and I also had been schoolmates together at the Manassas Industrial Colored School.

"I remember when black people couldn't even go to school in this town," the man told Thompson.

In another corner of the hall, some other half-drunk white man started talking about the O.J. Simpson verdict, Rodney King, the Million Man

March, and the sorry state of race relations in this country, prompting two obviously uncomfortable black women standing near him to find some place else to mingle.

At one point during the "victory" party, Bank's white campaign manager stood up to introduce his newly elected city leader as "not much of a public speaker, but a great candidate," while grins and nods of approval came from the crowd of about forty mostly white well-wishers, campaign workers, and media.

Banks smiled too, and I doubt seriously that he took the meaning of his handler's words the same way I did. The line hit me in an odd way: "The boy can't do nothing, but he's one of the good ones." The words raced through my head as though they had been spoken aloud. I looked away, trying to hide my uneasiness.

When it came time for our new mayor to speak, he did so awkwardly, stumbling haphazardly in his attempt to conjure up the proper words—the ones that thanked God for his good fortune and the ones that tried to explain in his own unique way how he ever got the notion to run in the first place. He thanked a young white girl, about ten years old, and who stood at the back of the room, for being one of his youngest supporters during the campaign; then he pointed out a young white boy in the crowd and joked that the two had decided to become fishing buddies. George Banks was all smiles, all proud.

"Read the speech I gave you," urged the campaign manager in an impatient, embarrassed tone. Banks eagerly complied, reading word for word from the prepared script in his hands. He read about how he would push for the building of a new high school, a campaign promise of his, as the crowd applauded its approval.

When Banks finished, the campaign manager snatched the speech from his hands and quickly shuffled it to a waiting reporter.

I left the party feeling torn. I had voted for Banks, as had most blacks in town, and there was something gratifying about seeing a black face occupying the town's highest office—if for no other reason than to know that it was possible. But I couldn't help but reflect on the old saying as I took one last look at George Banks and his circle: The more things change the more they stay the same.

I discovered racism in that Southern town at thirteen, faced with having to leave my home to get a high school education in a town more than an hour away. It has been my constant companion ever since. At thirteen you should not have to worry about getting the basics in life—an education, a safe environment—as if you are locked in a life-and-death struggle. But that's the South, and as I would later learn, that's also America. A lot of my early experiences have left deep wounds, the kind you would rather not discuss. Instead you learned to suppress them as if hoping that they were merely bad dreams and not your reality. Recently I picked up a book written by someone who I knew could relate to my feelings, and to borrow from her account of life as one of the nine students to integrate the public schools in Little Rock, "warriors don't cry."

My autobiography is not just an accounting of a life that has taken me from the Virginia farms to the White House to the Great Wall of China. It is my journal of what life does to a person and what can be learned from it. It is also history—of a town, of a people—that continues to be written. Every day we open our newspapers or turn on the television and see a world where solutions to problems seem harder to come by. This book is no panacea; it is one man's story, my story, my community's story, my people's story.

Chapter One
Warren County Warriors

The black elementary school in Front Royal, Virginia, went up to the seventh grade. After that it was understood that if we wanted to go to a high school, our parents would have to send us away to live at the colored boarding school sixty miles away in Manassas or to the other colored school in Berryville, about twenty-five miles away. It was just a fact of life in the 1950s when I was growing up.

The big school in our town, Warren County High School, was all white in those days, and there was no high school for blacks in the county. So when my time came, the school board sent me to live at the Manassas Industrial Colored School. The school didn't cost anything because it was a public school, and the school board picked up the tab.

I was only thirteen years old in 1955, leaving home for the first time, when my father drove me to the school some sixty miles from Front Royal. It was strange knowing that I would have to live there and that I couldn't go home at the end of the day. A lot of the parents who brought their kids to the school had to leave them there. Most didn't have cars, so if the kids wanted to get home at all they had to hitchhike. The year I started, my father went to the Warren County school board and made them provide a bus so the kids from Front Royal could at least go home every two weeks.

I didn't know much about the school when I went there, didn't know its history. In fact I hadn't even thought to go back there as an adult until I began writing this book. When I stepped from my car at the site of the old school, it was as if I had stepped back in time. The buildings—the classrooms and the dormitories—are long gone, replaced by concrete outlines where they once stood. All that remains is the massive stone archway leading into the Carnegie Building, where we took most of our lessons. There is also a scale model on the site made of bronze showing the locations of the original buildings and a kiosk with pictures and a recording of the history, narrated by Lark McCarthy, who does local newscasts in Washington.

A lot of people used to call it the Jennie Dean School after the woman who founded it in 1894. Jane Serepta Dean, known as "Jennie," was born a slave in Prince William County about 1852. She had no formal education herself but wanted to see black children get the same kind of education the white kids got. It was a private school until 1938, when the state figured it could be used for all of the black students in the region. It remained open as a segregated black facility until 1966. A modern elementary school now sits behind the old site, and it is also named for her.

I was assigned to the male dormitory and lived on the second floor. The room was nothing special, just a bed and bare walls. We had two rooms together with one door for four of us. To get to my room I had to go through somebody else's room. If you wanted to go to the bathroom you had to go downstairs. We had a dean to supervise us; he occupied two rooms downstairs with his family.

We ate our meals in the girls' dormitory just across the lawn from us. The last meal ended at five o'clock, so by nine a lot of kids were hungry again. On Saturdays we only got two meals—breakfast and lunch—and then two sandwiches for the evening. If we were still hungry we would usually go into Manassas, but basically we just passed the time playing "bid whiz."

I made a few friends during the year I spent in Manassas, and there was this little girl who lived down the road from the school that I sort of had my eye on. But when you're new to a place it takes a while before you are really welcomed, and those of us in the dormitories were viewed as outsiders. There were some people I knew from my home town, those who continued their schooling. Other kids from my neighborhood went to schools in other states where they had families with whom they could stay.

Around 2 years old sitting on the steps of the family's first rented home.

You tended to stick with a group of kids your own age, and you stayed away from the older boys because they could get you into trouble. And besides, they didn't really want us youngsters around anyway. One time I saw this group of older boys sneaking over to the girls' dormitory to get some milk that was stored inside a cooler on the back porch. They knew how to pick the lock, and they would get in there pretty easily. Of course I'm just this little nosy kid and I yelled out to them, as they're crushing milk cartons and flushing them down the commode to hide the evidence, "Hey, what are you guys doing?"

And they shot back, "You better keep your mouth shut."

Believe me, I did—and they didn't offer me any of that milk either.

Another night they had this free-for-all. They cut off all the lights and started throwing bottles all over the place, just being typical, crazy teenagers. The next day the headmaster held a meeting to see if he could get us to tell who had done it.

Nobody told, and we were all punished. We had to stay in our rooms for two weeks, and we were all assigned to cleanup details for the same amount of time. The janitor, who normally took care of the cleanup, supervised us and got something of a break.

Another night a group of boys got caught inside the girls' dormitory on a midnight creep. They had taken a ladder to one of the windows, and the girls' dean caught them as they were coming back out.

When winter came, the pipes froze up and there was no water to drink, but at least there was an old Coca-Cola machine outside by the boys' dormitory. More than a few times I would see some of the older guys take pennies, filed down to the size of dimes, and drop them in the coin slot. Now that's one thing they did let me in on, and I drank a lot of Cokes that year.

With all of the harsh weather in Manassas that year I came down with a bad cold. I was small anyway—I couldn't have weighed more than ninety pounds—and my nose was bleeding every other night. When I came home at the end of the school year, I weighed less than eighty pounds and was so frail that my father didn't make me do any chores for two weeks.

My brother John was to join me in Manassas for the next school year, but after seeing what happened to me, my father went back to the school board and told them he wasn't going to send any more of his children to that place. He told them he wanted us to be home every night, so he got the school board to put a bus on the road so we could go to the colored school in Berryville.

So John and I ended up going to Johnson-Williams High School in 1956. We would catch the bus early in the morning and get home in time to finish milking the cows and to do other chores. Sometimes we would get back late, even after dark. One time there was a lot of snow on the ground and the bus ran off the road into a ditch. We didn't get home until 9:00 P.M. My father got real upset, but there wasn't much he could do because the school board was unconcerned about black students. We went to Johnson-Williams for two years.

We were treated like outsiders at that school, too. We couldn't participate in sports or go to dances because there was no activity bus to bring us home. My father really liked the arrangement, however, because he had another set of hands back on the farm. Gene, my youngest brother, wasn't old enough to do any chores yet.

For years we all just went along with segregation in the schools until we heard about Mr. Oliver Brown's case against the Topeka, Kansas, Board of Education in 1954. When the Supreme Court ruled that the schools had to integrate, Virginia's governor at the time, a man named Thomas B. Stanley, organized what was called "Massive Resistance Law" as a way of legally ignoring the decision. Several states did that, including a defiant Georgia, which put the Confederate stars and bars on its state flag in protest.

Sometimes it's hard to explain to young people what it meant when you had the most powerful politicians in your state telling the whole world that it would destroy the country if I sat in a classroom with a white child. In those days they didn't use code words; their hatred of us was not hidden, and it was sanctioned by law.

By 1958, when my sister, Betty, was ready to go to high school, my father decided he'd had enough of sending his children miles away. It was bad enough having to send his sons out of town, but there was no way he wanted his thirteen-year-old daughter to be that far from home.

Every year the school board gave the black parents enrollment cards for each child so they could decide what school to send us to—Manassas or Berryville. There were no other choices. When he got my sister's card, my father scratched out those choices and wrote in that he wanted to send her to Warren County High School. He argued that since his tax money was paying for it, his children had a right to go there. The school board naturally sent the card back, reminding him that colored children were not allowed to go to Warren County, but he just sent it right back to them like he had the first time.

Since my father was a member of the N.A.A.C.P., he called it for help. After a few meetings, it was decided that he would file a lawsuit against the school board in Betty's name. Oliver W. Hill—the first black lawyer I had ever seen—took the case. Mr. Hill and Thurgood Marshall, who would eventually become the first African-American to occupy a seat on the Supreme Court, were good friends. He was a striking presence, a big man, and he made black parents feel confident that the case could be won.

Mr. Hill's letter to the Warren County School Board came the same day the board decided to build the Criser School, a combination elementary and high school for colored children in Front Royal. One group of black parents, however, wanted no part of separate facilities. They had gotten tired of what white supremacy and white separatism had done to them and wanted that cycle to end with their children.

They also complained that their children were not treated well in Manassas or in Berryville and said that it was difficult for them to take part in P.T.A. activities because they were seen as outsiders by the local families. Others, especially those who had gone to those schools, took pride in sending their children there and saw it as a tradition.

On February 18, 1959, after getting out of the car with my sister Betty behind to make that long historic walk up the hill and steps of Warren County High School surrounded by policemen, F.B.I., and Security people.

We won the lawsuit pretty easily since Oliver Brown had paved the way and in plenty of time for the 1958 school year. But actually getting into Warren County High would take more doing. When fall came, the school board closed the schools. Many white leaders blamed blacks, saying that they should have just waited another year for the Colored school to open. Other whites said they had no problem with integration and that it did seem like black parents had a point. Some even said that while they didn't like the idea of integration they'd rather have that than no schools.

The new governor, a man named J. Lindsay Almond, Jr., stepped in next, using the Massive Resistance Law to shut schoolhouse doors. Of course white folks saw that coming and started private schools all over town for their children in churches, abandoned buildings, or wherever they could find the space. They raised money among themselves for the school with white business owners giving money and supplies.

The white students were pretty well split on the issue, though most of them favored segregation like their parents did. But they didn't lose much. For example, despite the fact that the school was closed, the white kids who were attending John S. Mosby Academy were allowed by the Virginia High School League to play Warren County's 1958 football schedule. They were also allowed to use public transportation to get to their private schools.

Newspaper articles at the time noted that for the white kids, private school was a lot of fun. Many whites didn't even bother going to class. Their attitude basically was that they could just ignore the "Negroes" and go on with their lives with their education funded by the Warren County Educational Foundation.

For a few months, we black students had no school to go to, but on December 1, 1958, our parents formed the Front Royal Educational Fund, which worked along with an educational group in Washington headed by Mrs. Burma Whitted, and enrolled twenty of us in their schools in Washington, D.C., and found families with whom we could stay. I was placed with Reverend Harold Carter and his family along with my brother, my sister, and three other kids. I was sent to Eastern High School, which ironically was already integrated. The irony didn't get by me: Before, I had to leave my home town to go to a segregated school; this time I was leaving home to go to an integrated school.

The move wasn't free. Tuition, which was paid by the education fund, was seventy-nine dollars for junior high school students and eighty-eight dollars for high school pupils. Room and board in the Washington homes was one hundred fifty-eight dollars for junior high kids and one hundred seventy-six dollars for high school students. Black parents at American Viscose, where my father worked, donated money when they could, and some of the students went to press conferences, rallies, and fund raisers to get support.

On February 10, 1959, Judge John Paul in Harrisonburg ruled that Warren County had to open schools to blacks, and we all went back home. A month earlier, the Virginia Supreme Court ruled that Massive Resistance was unconstitutional, but white folks weren't finished. The school board appealed to a Baltimore circuit court and offered to pay our tuition in Washington if we waited until September to reopen the schools. But Judge Simon E. Sabloff ignored that request, accused the school board of stalling, and ordered the schools back in session.

The night before our first day back to school someone shot at our house, scaring the dog so badly that he ran off dragging the doghouse behind him. My father found him the next day, still chained to the house.

February 18 was my first day at Warren County High. All I can remember is running into a gauntlet of white people lining the sides of the driveway heading up the hill to the school shouting out "nigger" and a barrage of other things I couldn't make out. A handful of white kids tried to go to school with us but were shouted down by the crowd and convinced to stay away.

That hill leading up to the school had always seemed steep to me, but on that day it seemed like Mt. Everest. At the bottom of the hill a white man named F. Brent Sandridge met with us to give us instructions on where to go once we entered the building. He told us to go directly to the auditorium, where we would meet our teachers. We appreciated it since none of us had ever been in the school before. Why he met us outside the school rather than waiting for us to get inside, I don't know. The cracking in his voice betrayed his nervousness as he shot glances at the screaming mob across the street.

Even back then I wondered why white folks were making such a fuss just because us black folks wanted to go to a school where we lived.

There were twenty-four that had actually enrolled to initiate integration of the Warren County High School System. Although it was anticipated that twenty-four would enroll, Samuel Fletcher never registered.

Twenty-three registered two days after school started, two students dropped out. Elizabeth Dean did so to attend cosmetology school. Joyce Henderson decided not to attend and went back to school in New York.

By this time there were twenty-one of us left from the original group of twenty-three. For the first few days our parents car-pooled all of us to the bottom of the hill and let us off there to walk up as a unified group. During this time only the students and staff were allowed on the schools property. After that we started riding a blacks-only school bus, driven by Rudolph "Pete" Sloane. I admit I was afraid, and I wondered if those kids at Central High in Arkansas I'd seen on television felt the same way. I never paid much attention to them until I was in their shoes.

The twenty-one of us were the only students that first year in a school building that was built for more than a thousand. Sometimes I would be one of only two students in a class. The whites refused to send their children back and decided to keep them in the private school until the end of the school year.

From February to June it was actually pretty nice for us. We got to know each other pretty well—we studied together, ate together, and played basketball in the gym. We also learned the layout of the school, which none of us had ever seen before from the inside.

The black students received no credit for the time we spent at Warren County without the white kids. The school board said we hadn't been there long enough to get any credit since we spent part of the year in Washington. We ended up having to repeat the entire year. The white kids, of course, got full credit for going to their private schools.

Reflecting recently, I came to truly appreciate the camaraderie, friendships, and group support of my classmates as I read about the experience of Clyde Kennard who, around this same point in history (1958), tried unsuccessfully to integrate Mississippi Southern College in Hattiesburg (now the University of Southern Mississippi). His lone efforts probably cost him his life. Once-secret records now revealed show that Mr. Kennard was wrongly imprisoned in 1959 to thwart his integration attempt just six years prior to the university being integrated. Mr. Kennard's situation may have had a different outcome had he known the same support which I was fortunate enough to have enjoyed. I see him as a lone pioneer with a vision that was ahead of his time.

Only half of the white students came back to Warren County High in the fall of 1959. The others continued to go to Moseby Academy. The Criser School for colored students had opened by then, and all of the black students who had gone to Manassas and Berryville had gone there. The twenty of us were still the only blacks at Warren County.

We all rode the school bus together—the Warren County blacks and those who went to Criser. The twenty of us were treated as pariahs by the other students. They called us "high-class niggers" and "white people lovers" and wanted little to do with us. We all sat together and tried to

June 8, 1961 One of the proudest days in my life was to donned that cap and gown holding that diploma knowing that the struggle for achieving a high school education had come to an successful conclusion and that it had opened the door for others to follow.

ignore the taunts. We soon realized that we were outcasts in both the black and white communities.

It began to get harder for us in school. We had to learn our "dos" and "don'ts"—like not going into the bathroom alone because the white kids would taunt and threaten us if they could isolate us. Suddenly everywhere we went inside the school was the same as it had been walking up that hill, the same name-calling, the same abuse. And while we all wanted to get even, we knew we had to keep our tempers and try to stay out of trouble.

The people in D.C. had told us how to deal with the press during their many lectures with us, how to act when people tried to do things to us, and how not to say anything back to the teachers no matter what they accused us of doing. There was to be no back talk, and if a reporter asked us something we would just say "no comment" and move on. We knew the world was watching us.

We had trouble with some of the white teachers who had never had to deal with black students. One teacher, Mrs. Czarnitzki, was an older woman who taught the English class. She always watched me and would accuse me of cheating off some white kid's work. My father went in and talked to her on several occasions. I knew she was a racist, but I didn't say anything to her, and I made sure I knew my lesson, made sure she knew I didn't need to cheat.

When I went to the Manassas school, I had an English teacher who couldn't teach a lick, and that year I didn't learn a thing. All I remember is that he made us write the word *idiosyncrasy* five hundred times. English got no easier at Warren County. In general I was a C student, but I had a couple of Bs. I liked math, and I was pretty good at it. I can't say that I thought I was smarter than the white kids, but I knew I was just as smart.

Frank Grier, who was in the same year of school as myself, had a new car to drive each year, so we had transportation if we wanted to go hang out after class. The white kids didn't like that at all and would ask each other—just loud enough for him to hear— "How could a nigger afford a new car like that?" Some folks would even ask him to his face.

Not everyone at the school was nasty. Actually there were some pretty nice people, too, like the Seal brothers. Virgil Seal was pretty popular with the white girls, and he had this unique kind of hair style that had the girls calling him Elvis. Virgil was in a few of my classes, and he would initiate a conversation or two with me from time to time.

"Kilby," he said, "I just want you to know that I am going to talk to you no matter what other folks around here think of it. I don't care. People are people in my mind."

We stayed friends until graduation, and it seemed like he was one of the few white people who was glad to see me graduate. I never saw him again after that. A few years later I heard that he had been killed in a car crash.

But he was rare. Most of them muttered "nigger" or "damned fool" or something more colorful, or they'd try to push us into doing something. It was near the end of my senior year, a few days before graduation, when things seemed to heat up. I had driven my dark blue 1953 Ford up to the school and was sitting in it waiting for John to come out. The car had a nice shine on it that day, and I was just leaning back, window open, enjoying the breeze.

"That's that goddamned Kilby boy," I heard some white boy say to another standing behind the car.

"We ought to kick his black ass," his friend chimed in, spitting on the back of the car.

I knew they were baiting me, and I wanted a piece of them. But I was also two days away from graduation, and I had come too far to let a fight with some white boys mess that up.

There were only three blacks in my graduating class in 1961—me, Faye Coleman, and Frank Grier—and we were to be the first black graduates. One girl, Anne Rhodes, who was a year older than us, was supposed to have graduated a year earlier, but she didn't have the credits. Faye got scared and dropped out to marry a minister's son, leaving just me and Frank.

The minister, a real light-skinned man with grey eyes who was loved by some white people, didn't believe in integration, refused to send his kids to Warren County, and told people my father was crazy. We always believed that he pressured Faye into dropping out. He eventually moved to another county. There were a lot of people who were too afraid to participate, and he was one of them.

A lot of people tried to discourage Frank and me from going on, but I knew I had to do it because my father was the leader. And because there were two of us, Frank and I supported each other.

The entire time I spent in that school had been a trying experience for me. The white people were after my father for all the trouble they believed he had caused them, and being his children, John, Betty, and I knew we had to stand strong.

The night riders had been coming by the house from the beginning. My father kept the upstairs windows partially open, so if he saw somebody messing around the house he could just point the barrel of his gun out and start shooting. That's where the kids slept. He listened closely every time a car would pass by. If he would hear one stop, he sprang out of bed and waited to hear if a door slammed, meaning that somebody had gotten out and was heading toward the house. If that happened, he would wait until they were halfway into the yard before turning on the porch light, which would chase them away.

Other times people would call us up on the phone, then hang up as soon as we'd answered or yell "nigger" into the phone before hanging up.

One morning there was a bloody sheet hanging over the mailbox. My father didn't want to remove it himself because he thought there might have been a bomb or something inside. He called the sheriff, but you can't get fingerprints off a sheet, so we never knew who did it. Then a couple of our cows were poisoned, and we had to destroy a calf whose front legs had rotted and whose bones had broken through the skin because someone had taken rubber bands and fastened them around its ankles to cut off circulation.

The dog we had for protection was so mean that sometimes he bit us. One night we had him tied up to a post outside. He began barking, and my father ran upstairs to the window to see what was happening. The next thing we knew somebody was shooting at the house. Seeing where it was coming from, he fired back. We heard somebody fall over the fence trying to get away. By the next day, we knew who the guy was because he ended up in the hospital with a broken leg. After that, somebody poisoned the dog.

Another day, while my father was at a church meeting and my mother was alone with the children, somebody else shot toward the

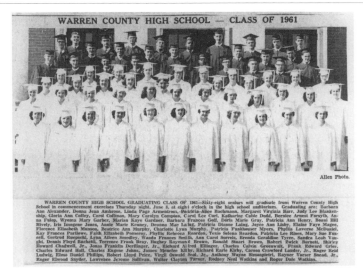

1961-First integrated graduating class picture of Warren County H.S. with sixty-eight seniors.

house. My mother saw the bullet whiz by the window while she was washing dishes. At first all she saw was a flash of light. Then it registered. My brother and I would ride into town with my father whenever he went there, and we stuck close to him. I guess he felt like even they wouldn't go so far as to try to kill a man in front of his children, although a few years later the N.A.A.C.P. field secretary Medgar Evers was shot in Jackson, Mississippi, while his children witnessed the incident. My father had never owned a shotgun before these things started happening.

After going through all of that, by the time graduation came, to tell you the truth, I was a mess. The last thing I truly remember was sitting there with my class, waiting. I don't remember much about that night. I know I walked across the stage, and I know I saw a sea of angry white people, but everything else was an unreal blur. My legs were weak, and I felt like I was falling to pieces on the inside from all the turmoil.

There was a lady who did volunteer work for the N.A.A.C.P. who lived about three miles down the road from us; her name was Catherine Butler. She had a station wagon and made sure all of us had a ride to her house where a graduation celebration was being held in our honor that night. Later we were invited to Atlantic City to be honored for our accomplishments; I guess you could say we had become famous.

That same year—1961—after the success of the initial integration effort had resulted in two black graduates from Warren County High School, more black parents began petitioning to get their children into Warren County High and the other white schools in town. The time had come for Front Royal to desegregate its elementary schools, and I had played a part in history.

The day after graduation I went back to work. I had a job in Falls Church, Virginia, which is where I'd worked for a couple of summers. A few of the fellows who also worked out that way would meet in Front Royal and then car pool to Falls Church. I usually drove my father's car to work, but on this day I rode with some other people.

On the second day after graduation my father was there to greet me when I got back to Front Royal. He told me that the sheriff had been to the house and wanted to arrest me for throwing rocks at some white boys.

The day before graduation—and the day after the two white boys spat on the car—these two other white boys, James Kenneth Hamilton and Donald Lee Ritenour, were riding their bicycles up the road near our house. I knew Hamilton from high school. He had threatened me a couple of times in the boys room, and he was one of those mean-type white boys. Ritenour attended the white John S. Mosby Academy.

As they passed, words were exchanged, and Gene started throwing rocks at them. I was in the house when it all started, but when I came out, saw my brother and Gene, then saw those white boys, I was reminded of the school bathroom threats, and I grabbed a couple of rocks and started throwing at them, too. They rode away, but I wasn't through with them. I jumped in the car with John and a friend, and we followed those boys and started yelling at them out the window.

We purposely left Gene at home, not wanting him to get in any trouble. At the time we didn't know what had started the rock throwing, but years later Gene told me that the white boys had called him "nigger" as they rode by.

"You're not at Warren County High now!" I screamed at those white boys, three years of rage exploding from me before I finally had my fill and turned around to go back home. The white boys came back by our house after us later on, but by then we had gone inside.

When my father met me, he told me the police had a warrant and wanted to search the farm for me, but since the name on the warrant said James Kilby, my father looked at them and replied, "I'm James Kilby; what do you want?" They later gave him a contempt citation for not cooperating. He was convicted at first, but the conviction was later overturned on appeal.

My father had already called the N.A.A.C.P.'s lawyers before he came to get me, and they said the best thing for me to do was to go down to the courthouse and turn myself in. Otherwise the police would have waited until about midnight or so and come and gotten me out of my bed and forced me into custody. We went down to the court house, the police charged me with disorderly conduct, and they wanted to put me in jail.

But my father spoke up and said, "If you put him in a cell, you're going to have to put me in the cell, too."

He made sure that the minister was there with us, Reverend Herman Frank. Reverend Frank, hearing what my father said, also spoke up and said, "And if you put them in jail, you may as well put me in jail with them."

The police saw that those two men were serious and allowed me to post a two-hundred-and-fifty-dollar bond. They both knew what would happen if they had left me in there that night, and there was no way they were going to walk away and let that happen.

A couple of days later I was brought into court to face charges, but they also brought in Frank Grier, the other black graduate, and charged him. It was all over the *Northern Virginia Daily* newspaper. "Two Warren Negroes Charged in Attack on White Youths."

The article went on to describe the incident this way:

> Deputy Sheriff E.L. Merchant said the attack on the two white youngsters occurred on Wednesday between 11 A.M., and 1 P.M. The white boys, both small, were identified as [Hamiton and Ritenour]. The deputy quoted the white youngsters as saying that they jumped on their bicycles and rode away, hoping to elude the Negroes. However, the Negroes put [their] automobile in reverse and chased them back, the boys said. The boys [said] that they did manage to escape, however, and that they went fishing.

Problem was that Frank wasn't even there when it happened; that's where the police made their mistake; they were clearly trying to punish both of us for graduating from Warren County High School! In court Frank obviously was found not guilty. Then they turned around and issued my brother John a bench warrant. Of course they found me guilty, though, and gave me a fifty-dollar fine and a one-year sentence.

Before I graduated, I passed the air force enlistment test. It seemed like a good job opportunity. I was intrigued by flying, and, because I scored a ninety-five on the administrative test, I figured I had a good chance to get into an airplane. According to the sentence they gave me, however, I was not eligible to join the air force until a year after I graduated. I didn't have to go to jail, but I couldn't go into the air force as I had planned.

The lawyer and my father together made a quick tactical decision to get me out of town to avoid testifying against my brother. I suddenly moved to Washington, D.C., while the summons was sent to my father's house.

Because no money was sent to cover traveling expenses for my return to a Front Royal court as required by law for out-of-town witnesses summoned to testify, the lawyer advised me not to return from Washington unless the money was provided. When my brother went to trial, and I

June 8, 1996 The day of the 35th anniversary interview June 8, 1996 this racial epithet was seen on the corner wall of Warren County H.S. This gives you reason to wonder if the attitude and the mindset will ever change.

wasn't there, they couldn't prosecute him because they had no one who could identify him at the scene except me.

I didn't mind leaving because I felt like I was protecting my brother. To tell you the truth, I was sort of passing onto him what my father gave me—freedom from a night in jail.

The main thing was protecting my brother; we were close. When you get up with someone every day at four thirty in the morning you get that way. We did things together. We had to depend on each other. As we got older, we grew apart a little, but when I got remarried in 1995 I surprised him when I asked him to be my best man. He didn't know I still thought of him that way.

Later they tried to keep John from going back to Warren County High, but my father got a judge to order the school to let him in. Frank Grier died of pneumonia in 1970, nine years after we graduated I went to his funeral. I wish he was still here.

I didn't return to Warren County High until 1989, when a local television station decided to do a story on the thirtieth anniversary of the enrollment of the school's first black students. I have only been back one other time since.

As quickly as I had left Front Royal, I suddenly decided to return in September 1995 to care for my elderly parents after my father suffered a stroke.

Chapter Two
Front Royal in Black and White

Like I said before, the nickname "Helltown" meant something different for the blacks and whites who lived in Front Royal. For whites the name harkened back to the more wide-open, early frontier days, when pioneering men would come to town for their Saturday night romps—many of which ended in knockdown, drag-out fights.

Local historians like to talk about a French Huguenot named Peter Lehew, the town's original namesake, who traveled to the American colonies to escape religious and political persecution. From Lehewtown the name of the area somehow evolved to Royal Front before becoming Front Royal. But for many the Helltown moniker stuck in local lore.

For black folks Helltown came to symbolize another kind of fight, one that never seems to end. I did not realize the significance of the town's nickname to me until I recounted the hell I suffered during the integration experience in a story about my father published in the February 6, 1986, edition of the *Washington Post* newspaper.

I was born April 13, 1942, in Flint Hill, Virginia, to James Wilson Kilby, a janitor and farmer, and Catherine Elizabeth Kilby, who raised us. I am the oldest of five children, including John, Betty, Patricia, and Gene. John was always a big sport; he loved to look good and drive big cars. He was flamboyant. Even though we worked summers in Falls Church to make money, he was always broke. If he saw a suit that he wanted that cost $39.95 and he had forty dollars, that suit was his. He'd bring his suit home, dress up, and look real good, but he wouldn't have a dime left. So, of course, he'd go to our father and ask for five dollars.

My father would ask, "Well, John, didn't you work this week?" John would say he spent it all on a suit or something, and so my father would say no. Then John would go on about how it was our father's job to look out after us until we were twenty-one, or whatever he thought would work, and my father would just give up and give it to him.

But that was John. In high school he was one of those students who didn't have to study while I was struggling in the same courses. When he took the SAT test, he got a high score and decided he wanted to go to Fisk University in Nashville. He was the first in our family to go to college. He worked hard that summer and saved about three hundred dollars, but when it was time to go to school, he had spent all the money on clothes and such and didn't even have enough money to get on the bus.

So he really started working on my father then, and he was a soft touch because he really wanted John to go to college. He gave him the money, John went to Nashville and studied hard for the first few months, and then he started fooling with the girls and having fun and his grades came down.

John was always short of money, and he couldn't understand why our father never had enough to give him as it seemed the other parents did for their children. But what John didn't understand was that those folks' parents were doctors and lawyers, and our father was a janitor who had a little farm. So he sold his blood, and one year he decided to go out for the football team because he heard it paid fifteen hundred dollars. Except for little league baseball one summer, he had never played football or any other sport in his life.

He played about two years. The first year he got the wind knocked out of him; the next year a buddy of his on the team got hurt pretty badly, and that shook him up. He quit the team and started working. Today he manages a store and drives a Jaguar.

In 1991 he made history of a sort in Dade County when he and two other African Americans opened a Z-Mart, a black-owned department store in Liberty City, Florida. When the Ames department store closed its doors in 1990, about one hundred people were left unemployed, and the local residents were left without a place to shop. John and his partners Charles Howze and Joan Davidson pooled their resources—going for about a year on the charity of family members while they raised the money. To secure a loan, they put their houses up as collateral. All three of the partners had been managers at various times at the old store.

Their store had a definite black theme—red, yellow, and green stripes along the walls and African designs and products geared toward black people. They were written up in the Congressional Record on September 11, 1991, when Florida Congresswoman Ilena Ros-Lehtinen applauded them as the first black department store in the Miami area.

I wasn't as close to Betty as I was to John. But I think that as the center of the lawsuit that opened up the high school, she felt a certain sense of pride knowing that she was part of something that significant; she knew it made my father happy. She was quiet when she was a little girl. She eventually earned a master's degree.

Patricia was very young when we were going through all of the changes with the school. To tell the truth, I really didn't get to know her until she moved to Washington and enrolled at Howard University. She had an apartment there with about two or three roommates. Patricia was very studious; she also earned a master's degree.

Gene was feisty; we always said he was just spoiled. Whereas John and I had to milk the cows by hand, there was an electric milking machine by the time he came along. He was also the only one for whom our parents bought a car. Like Patricia he went to Howard, and like John he played football. I really only became close to him after he was a grown man. He has always pretty much kept to himself.

I always had a sense of myself as the big brother, and I always knew what was expected of me. I went to Gene's games at Howard. I always believed in saving because I had this dream of one day owning a house. Because of this I didn't go out a whole lot, and on the few times I did, it seemed like I went out with an older group.

We grew up on a sixty-acre farm and raised milk cows, chickens, and pigs. We had a daily routine on the farm, especially after I turned nine years old; getting up every morning and milking about two or three cows. I'd get up about four-thirty in the morning, and after that we'd feed the cows, wash up, eat breakfast, and catch the bus for school at seven-thirty. That was most days, but about two days a week, we would have extra chores. We had to set the full milk cans out by the road so the milk truck could pick it up; that's how my father earned extra money.

In the evening after school, we would go to the refrigerator and grab a snack, put on our work clothes again, and milk the cows for the evening. Then it was time to get ready for dinner, eat, do our homework, and get to bed. I had the responsibility of cleaning out the barn, and I had to get to bed early in order to be able to get up the next morning.

My father was my one real role model. When he was a child, he and his parents worked as servants in the home of a wealthy white family in Rappahanock County. The experience shaped him in a profound way. He has always been a deep thinker and a man who was big on responsibility, whether it was chores or homework. If we got out of line, we knew he would let our backsides have it, and "wait until your father gets home" was a well-worn cry from my mother.

James W. Kilby was the community's activist. He founded the 4-H Club, and he was a deacon at Macadonia Baptist Church in Flint Hill, Virginia, and always made sure to drive us to Sunday School. It was our family's church. He kept school buses on the road for black children to get to Manassas and Berryville. He built the house we lived in. When I was thirteen, he talked to me about being a Christian, and a year later, on July 15, 1956 I joined the church.

After winning the school battles, my father moved onto other causes in our community. He led pickets of the Safeway and A & P grocery stores, the Tastee Freeze diner, and McCrory's five and dime to get them to hire blacks who had been denied jobs. He later spoke out against discrimination in state government and public school hiring. He then went on to serve on school committees and job-training boards, and created a home weatherization program for low-income residents. At one point he even formed a nonprofit company that built brick houses for black families.

My mother, Catherine, ran the house. In general she didn't bother anybody and she didn't want anybody to bother her. She didn't trust white people and treated them with respect only when respect was shown to her. She didn't always agree with what my father was doing and wasn't into politics or the Civil Rights movement. She cut my hair until I was eleven and bought or made my clothes for me until I was twelve. She became the first black to be employed at the local McCrory's store.

My parents still live on the same grounds, though they built themselves a new brick house next to the old one, which they now rent out. The residents in the old house are white, which I sometimes find amusing when I think of that building's history.

My parents have always led by example. They didn't smoke, didn't drink, and were nonviolent; they made me what I am. People say that those values may be too straight-laced and may think that there is something wrong with not putting up with "foolishness."

There was not a whole lot of outside stuff for us to do in Front Royal. There was no time for that, just time for the chores. It seemed that our family was the only one that really had to work like mules. The rest of the kids I got on the bus with had homes with little yards, and that was about it. One friend had a job delivering the *Grit* newspaper, and other than the Pines brothers who worked in Falls Church with us, I don't know any of them who worked until we started working in Falls Church. My life was built on work; that's how it was structured.

Our family's first milk cow was Daisy. She was the cow on whom my brother John and I had to learn to milk. Our father challenged us, promising one dollar to the one who learned how to milk this cow first first—an incentive. Technically, we both learned at the same time, so he gave us both a dollar. That was how he got started raising cows; he would eventually have eleven cows. A bull came later on after we had seven or eight cows. Before that my father would take Daisy over to a neighbor's farm to be bred.

We ate a lot of beef and pork. My father had a system: One year he would kill the hogs and we would have mostly pork, and the next year he killed the steer and we had mostly beef. One year he killed four hogs, and since the family didn't eat chitlins, we'd give that away. The neighbors would come by and pick up tubs full, and they would be so grateful. My mother never cooked them in her kitchen, and we wouldn't eat those stinking things. We did sample them one time at a church dinner, but I didn't like them.

The next year my father bought a steer, fattened him up, and killed him. We were eating filet mignon and didn't even know it. My mother always had three square meals on the table, and we always had plenty to eat because we raised everything—the chickens, for the eggs, the cows, for the milk.

I can't really say it was fun for me growing up. It seemed like it was all work all the time. We all learned to be responsible, but we didn't do the things the other kids did like going fishing or hunting.

Happy Creek, the name of the area we lived in, was a close-knit community. Several of the families were involved in the civil rights movement, and we were there to support one another. I guess I was closest to the Pines family, mostly because Archie and Matthew Pines were close to my age and we got our driver's licenses at about the same time. Both of them had been part of that original group of nineteen students.

I used to look forward to the holidays because we would take a break from our chores and get together with other folks. Easter meant the Easter picnic and my one time all year to play softball. We would always gather in Elizabeth Furnace Park in the mountains and play ball, swim in the creek, and lounge under the pavilion. At Christmas time, we would have to learn a poem for the annual pageant and practice Christmas songs with Reuben Barbour banging away on the piano.

Rainy days were usually down times. Usually John and I would go visit Archie and Matthew, which was okay with our parents since they were boys. Visiting some of the other homes—and the daughters—had to be done discreetly so as not to arouse the parents' suspicions that we were up to no good.

Every now and then there was some room for fun. I remember one time when the pond froze over and we went for a sleigh ride on it, but really, we were busy all the time. Other times, like if there was a church picnic, we would get to play softball. We would go to the park up in the mountains.

The town of Front Royal was a typical small Southern town, divided up along racial lines. You would go into the banks and there would be no black tellers; you would go to the department stores, like J.J. Newberry's, and see no black salespeople; and you knew not to sit at the lunch counter. Every so often we would read about some young brothers who got into fights for trying to get served. The only time I saw a black in any of those types of stores was a seamstress in a clothing store. And the schools were segregated, so we didn't know very many of the white kids our age.

Warren County was not immune from slavery, and Front Royal was a slave town. Several white families owned Africans, but early on, black people were free and owned land here. Unfortunately there were several

June 8, 1996, the 35th anniversary of the first two black graduates. Interview conducted on the porch of Warren County High School by Patricia C. Hsu (Reporter) TV3 Harrisonburg, VA.

laws on the books designed to make sure that freedom was limited. One law, passed in 1801, made it illegal for free blacks to leave the county; if they did they could be bonded into slavery. Five years later the 1806 Removal Law was passed, stating that any blacks freed after that year had to leave Virginia.

Limestone mining in the nearby Luray Caverns became a big industry in the 1950s, and blacks managed a few jobs. There also was a demand for blacksmiths, shoemakers, and other craftspeople, and black folks found work. By the end of the Civil War, Virginia finally recognized black marriages as legal—something that had not been possible before. Not knowing where to go, many of the freed slaves stayed in the area in a section called Browntown.

In the 1880s, the Free Mill Benevolent Society was formed by black Front Royal residents, and Benevolent Hall was built. It became a central meeting place for the community. Taking advantage of the Reconstruction, fourteen blacks voted in the 1888 election and celebrated Benjamin Harrison's victory in the presidential race.

There is this one place in downtown Front Royal we have always known as "Free Town." That's not its real name, but it's a small neighborhood, mostly on Osage Street. Most black businesses had begun moving there early in the century, and by the 1940s, Osage became the black downtown. There was one little black-owned restaurant called the Cozy Ace, and another one called Tyler's. A few hundred feet down the street there is this old building that used to be owned by Haywood Timbers that had a pool hall in it and a barber shop. He drove a cab too.

Robertson Hall is where the American Legion would meet, and not too far from that is the Elks' Home. The barbershop was run by my uncle, the Reverend Carter Alsberry, pastor of Mt. Vernon Baptist Church for thirty-one years and my mother's brother. We'd go in there a lot when we went to town; he had operated the shop for several years.

Recently the town of Front Royal was awarded a grant to revitalize the Osage Street community. The grant was intended to cover the costs of new storm drains, new sidewalks, and wider streets. Some of the money also was intended to help homeowners refurbish their properties. The award money was refused by the town because it was not enough to fully complete the entire project. The town plans to reapply in the future for a larger grant to accomplish all the related work.

There really weren't a whole lot of heroes in Front Royal, nobody who inspired great awe. Reverend J.P. Baltimore was one, though. Besides pastoring at the Mt. Morris Church in Hume, Virginia, he had a Sunday morning radio program, and The Heavenly Gospel chorus sang on the show.

At the St. Paul Church there were a lot of folks who I respected. There was Deacon Harrison Dean, the Sunday school superintendent. We all used to laugh at the way he sang in church—kind of humming, like he was getting in touch with the ancestors. He was a short guy, clean-cut, tan complexioned. Reuben Barbour was another. He played the piano for the Mt. Nebo Church choir, and he always was practicing when I saw him. He was a strong, tough man, always in command. He served thirty years in the army and got wounded in one of the wars. He would whip us singers into shape for the Christmas pageants.

My pastor at the Macedonia Baptist Church in Flint Hill, Virginia, was someone else whom I admired. Reverend Thomas Proctor was my pastor from the time I joined the church at age fourteen until I moved to Washington, D. C., in 1961. Reverend Proctor was not only a dedicated preacher who performed my parents' marriage ceremony, but he was also a skilled carpenter and mason. His work as a mason lives on in the stonework of the historic Warren County courthouse building in Front Royal—the same courthouse where I received my one-year sentence for the rock-throwing incident.

Ressie Jeffries was the principal of the elementary school I attended. The elementary school was named in her honor. When the Ressie Jeffries Elementary School was converted to school administrative offices, the former black school, Criser High School, which opened in September, 1959, was renamed in 1976 for Mrs. Jeffries. Mrs. Jeffries was strict. She took no stuff off students, and you did not want to get called in front of her and have to face that paddle. I never got called in myself. She and her husband, lived in Front Royal, just down the hill from the Criser school, like most of the men in town, worked at the American Viscoe factory. They made rayon and nylon fabrics. Everybody worked there; my father did too.

Charles Washington was the big celebrity in town. We all used to call him "Chinky," and he was one of my Boy Scout leaders, the other was Henry Johnson. Chinky had a radio show on Saturday nights. The black music he played was all we heard because all the other stations played was country and western music. Except late at night, if the radio could pick it up, we could listen to some black music from an out-of-town station.

Out where I lived, in Happy Creek, was roughly five miles from downtown. The townspeople used to tease us about the name, joking that all we did out there was get happy and jump in the creek. Most people in our neighborhood were poor. The streets were very narrow, and there were no sidewalks. When I got a little older and could drive, my brother and I would go into town and hang out. I only went to the Elks' Home a couple of times, but I stopped because it seemed like people were always getting into some kind of a fight. We would still go back to that part of town, however, because it really was the only place to go.

There was one man in Free Town who was the only black notary public in town; he operated a convenience store out of the closed-in back porch of his home. His name was Enooh Cove. We all knew that he also sold bootleg liquor. He always drove a new car. His son was in the Boy Scouts with me and John, and he would drive us all to this summer camp. Eventually the police caught up with him, confiscated his car, then raided his house and found bottles of liquor stashed behind the walls.

We didn't go into Free Town a whole lot as children, mostly because we didn't have much time and also because it could get rough there. When we were old enough to drive, we would go into town and meet the girls. Now John liked to go to the pool hall, and sometimes I'd go with him. One night he got into it with this one fellow; they got to fighting, and the fellow threw a cue ball at John and hit him in the head. We were lucky to get out that night.

There was one movie house in Front Royal, and everybody went—black and white—but those were the days of segregation, so we had to sit in the balcony. I went there only twice in my life, I think, and my uncle John H. Kilby, Jr., took me both times. The rules were different in Washington, though. I remember going to a movie house in Washington years later and going automatically to the balcony, only to be told that we couldn't sit up there.

The atmosphere for blacks in Free Town was better than in the rest of Front Royal, but that doesn't mean white folks left us alone there either. One time there was this man who was half drunk, and he was just sort of staggering down the street not bothering anybody. The police came up on him and said something, and one of the officers put his hand on the guy's arm. All he did was brush the hand off, but the next thing I know the two cops had unbuckled their blackjacks and began beating him over the head. The man didn't die, but I don't know what happened to him.

I really didn't like going to that area after that incident; it just left a bad taste in my mouth. It did make me think about how I would react. I used to tell myself that I would take the beating, and, if I lived through it, the next time I saw them again I would have my gun, and I would walk up behind them and shoot them in the backs of their heads.

I was about six when I discovered I needed glasses. I couldn't see at all because my right eye was a droop-eye. I couldn't write straight. My teacher complained to my mother that I wrote diagonally across the page and slanted everything. I couldn't see big things. When I got the glasses I noticed the difference right away. Seeing for the first time was very different, but even with the glasses I couldn't quite get to twenty-twenty vision. I have never gone without glasses since, and I'd be lost if I tried.

At ten years old I worked for the white owners of a combination store and post office, and I would pull weeds from their vegetable and flower garden for fifty cents an hour. My father got me and my brother that job. We only had to walk ten minutes to their store, and we would only work half a day. Most times this was in the summer, and if the weather was clear the whole week you could make as much as ten dollars. The white lady, Mrs. Jennings, was real nice, she was a school teacher. We started working about nine o'clock, and at about eleven she would give us a break and bring each of us a Nehi soda and some cupcakes. Sometimes she'd even give us a pint of ice cream that we would split. Those grape Nehi sodas were good and made the work enjoyable.

Mrs. Jennings was the head of the household because Mr. Jennings liked the bottle. So we didn't have to worry about him because, technically, Mrs. Jennings was our boss. I mean, he would help out with the chores and all, but she was the one with whom we had real contact.

My father didn't really tell us why we were going to work. He just said, "I got a job for you." I assume it was because since it was summer he did that to keep us busy; of course, back then you just did what you were told anyway. You didn't really question what your parents said—at least we didn't.

My father was in charge in the community, too. He was the president and founder of the local 4-H Club that I joined as a kid. It was the Colored 4-H Club, according to the newspaper that came and took our picture. They had me take my glasses off for the picture, I recall.

Anyway in the 4-H Club they gave everybody pigs, and we were supposed to raise them. We learned everything about them—the first thing we learned was how to castrate the male pigs because, I suppose, they wanted to keep the pigs from getting into something. So my brother and I had my pig; I fed it, was responsible for it, and got it to the fair, where I won a second-place blue ribbon for it. I had a sow, and when she had little pigs my father sold them for me. After the first group he sold, he gave me twenty-five dollars, and that became my first savings account.

I got my second job working at a resort. This white man named Joseph Little saw me mowing our lawn and offered me a job working all day for him for eighty-five cents an hour. I worked with him for about four years. When the integration was approved by the Federal District Court in Harrisonburg, Virginia, in 1958, he was pressured by white people to fire all the black folks, but he wouldn't do it. He resigned, so we were forced to quit. We admired him for that. We considered him to be a very nice, fair-minded guy.

Chapter Three
Downstairs at the White House

I stayed in Washington after I was done with school and got a job with a company in Falls Church, Virginia, called Melpar. I was a porter at first, then got promoted to doing light assembly work at their operation in Bailey's Crossroads.

When I first got to Washington I moved back in with Reverend Harold Carter. I didn't stay there very long because Mrs. Carter took ill and soon died. I moved in with a cousin, Virginia, and her husband Ray Brown after that. She had just gotten married, so it was a little awkward having me around.

I had gotten so used to those early mornings that, after I left the farm and moved to Washington, D.C., it took some adjusting. When the sun started to come up I would try to lay there in the bed as long as I could, but I would feel real guilty about it. It took me a long time to get over that. Those city folks would stay in the bed and not get up until ten or eleven o'clock on a Saturday, and I personally thought it was a sin to stay in bed that long. But once I was in the city I didn't have to worry about milking cows twice a day, feeding chickens and hogs. Those days were hard, but after doing that I learned to appreciate hard work because life became easier for me as an adult.

By the time my year was up, I had changed my mind about the air force. I was bitter about having to wait that year and the way they treated me. I decided that I didn't want to shed even one drop of my blood for this country. I went to work with the State Department instead, working in the cafeteria busing tables and washing dishes.

It sounds like a contradiction, I guess, but I wasn't trying to get out of serving entirely, despite my anger, and actually I was inspired in part by President Kennedy. He was the first president I can remember. I admired his speeches and thought he was a man of courage; he made me rethink things. I wasn't old enough to vote for him since the voting age was twenty-one in 1960, but I would have voted for him.

In 1963 I went over to the C.I.A. to apply for a job. When I went there, I had on these tight pants, run over shoes, and was looking tacky. I took the test and did okay on all of it except the writing part, but luckily a white lady named Mrs. Hasel decided she would give me a hand.

She said to me, "You did all right, but I'm going to have to help you with the composition part. I want you to come back tomorrow wearing a suit and tie. I'm going to recommend you for a clerk's position."

I came back, but I wasn't sure if I would get the job because I had to take a polygraph test, and one of the questions they ask you is whether you have been arrested. I wasn't quite sure how I was going to answer that one given what had happened in Front Royal. It seemed like no matter what I did it was going to hurt my chances of getting the job. I couldn't lie because the machine would catch me, and I couldn't tell the truth because that would disqualify me.

But when I went over to Langley, Virginia, to take that test I believe the good Lord must have been watching over me. I just told them what had happened when they asked me the question. I gave them my explanation and told them about the circumstances. For some reason they didn't pay that any mind, and I got the job.

That incident did a lot for my confidence. It also taught me that if I did what I thought in my heart was right, if I was truthful, nobody could hurt me. I learned that I had to take a stand for what I believed in no matter what the cost. It seems funny that I would learn all of that from taking a lie-detector test, but I did.

My first assignment was in Alexandria, Virginia. After six months they wanted to assign me to an office across the street from the State Department. They didn't tell me, but I later learned that they wanted to promote this white guy because he had a bad fitness report with his white unit; he had been placed there to get his act together, and I was supposed to fill his job. He was the only white man in the group—even the supervisor was black. Now the supervisor was under pressure to give this guy a good review, and he resented it. He also resented me being used to fill this guy's old job, so he took me aside and told me that I should act like I couldn't do the job so they would have to keep the white guy there—that way he wouldn't get the promotion.

I was supposed to have one week's training. All we did was drive a van and make deliveries. It was actually a step down from my other job, where I had more responsibility. I listened to the supervisor and went through the week. Then I had to go up in front of someone else for another review. When this man asked me if I could handle the job I said, "No."

He said, "This is the only job I have for you." I told him I didn't believe that a place as large as the C.I.A. would have only one job opening.

The Jeep I drove for the commander of company D 163 Military Police unit of D.C. National Guard. It was used as a lead vehicle for the convoys also, as an escort vehicle for the firetrucks during the 1968 riots after Dr. Martin Luther King Jr. assassination

His face got kind of red. I guess he didn't appreciate what I had said, and he shot back, "This is the only job we have for you."

So I took the job.

When the Selective Service sent for me to go to Baltimore and take a physical and a written exam, I went and passed them. But this time I played it smart like the white boys and also signed up for the National Guard test. So rather than being drafted I ended up joining the D.C. National Guard; it was the best thing I'd ever done. I avoided the Vietnam War, just like Dan Quayle. I was in the Guard from 1964 to 1970.

I did my basic training at Fort Jackson, South Carolina. It lasted five months, and I was trained in field communications. When I came back to Washington they made me a military policeman. I would be on duty for the next six years—once a month on weekends and every year for two weeks at summer camp. My job was to chauffeur the captain of our unit.

Around the same time I was becoming a weekend warrior, I went back to the C.I.A. to see if there were any openings, but they had a hiring freeze in effect. I don't remember the name of the man in personnel who I talked to, but he told me at that time to call him back in two weeks and he would let me know if things had changed.

Meanwhile I got a job at Sears Roebuck pumping gas, but every two weeks I'd call that same man at the C.I.A. to see if anything had changed. After awhile he must have gotten tired of me calling. The man told me about this office the C.I.A. has on sixteenth Street that served as an employee pool. I asked what I had to do, and he said all I had to do was go there and wait until I was given an assignment. So I went there and signed up; I was there about a month.

You didn't really do anything when you were there, and your time was pretty much your own. I would see people just sitting around playing cards and just hanging out. It was strange for me because I was used to working every day. I didn't know there was a place you could go and get paid for not doing anything.

After I'd been there for about a month, one of the supervisors came by and told me that there was an opening at the White House and asked me if I would be interested. Of course I said yes. I remember feeling like I was six-feet tall because I was going to work in the home of the president. It was a pretty big deal for the family, too; to them it was a great achievement. Buddies in the neighborhood used to brag about it to make themselves sound big.

On my first day in the White House they gave me an information sheet telling me where to report. I didn't know anyone there and didn't really know what to expect. It took about three days before it hit me that this was where I worked.

I was like a lot of people who admired John Kennedy, and I admit it was a bit strange going to work there and realizing that he had died just a year before. My co-workers, those who had been there when Kennedy was alive, often talked about him. There also was a sense of confusion because there were people who wondered whether Johnson had anything to do with it, seeing as how the killing took place in Texas.

I was a messenger, and the job paid pretty well. I was to make deliveries to all of the government buildings, and we had to make sure to get a receipt for every letter we delivered. Somebody had to sign for it. My route included taking briefings to both national committee offices, the Pentagon, House and Senate offices, the cabinet offices, or some other place in the government. We went to the Capitol just about every day. I also got to deliver the president's State of the Union speech to Congress. We had to make sure there were enough speeches for each member.

There were five messenger drivers on my shift: me, Carol Strickland, Roscoe Brown, and Joe Brooks, who were black, and a white guy named Eaby, who was detailed to the White House from the army. Our shift ran from 9:00 A.M. to 5:30 in the afternoon. Every year we got new cars to drive; the government got them cheap, direct from the factory for only a dollar a year. They cost a lot less than those Pentagon hammers.

My car always had automatic transmissions, an AM/FM radio, air conditioning, and a CB radio. One year, my car had a tape deck. We easily had the nicest fleet among the government agencies. Most of the time I worked there we drove Fords, though a couple of times we had Dodges and Plymouths.

My CB code name was "Spud," given to me by one of my co-workers, John Green. My code number was thirty-five. After receiving my delivery assignment for the day, I would report out, "This is Spud Thirty-Five leaving the West Basement," to which they would reply, "Thirty-five, proceed." What I did at the White House was by no means a super high-level job, but it was honest work. Occasionally, I had the opportunity to drive Billy Dale, some years later became the travel office supervisor who was later fired in the travel scandal, to various meetings. For a country boy, the idea of serving the leaders of the free world was one I never took for granted because there are many people who never get the experience of walking inside that building. In many ways, being there helped me develop a much larger view of the world and a greater sense of what I could be.

Every so often we had to chauffeur some of the White House aides around town, but I rarely did that. One time President Johnson was supposed to be interviewed, and he didn't have any makeup, so I had to go to the store with one of his aides to get some pancake makeup and rouge and whatever for him.

When Johnson came in, he brought some of his people from Texas. There were two black guys, Eugene Williams and Samuel Wright. Wright's wife was Mrs. Johnson's personal aide. With those people working there we sort of had a connection to the president because they would talk about the girls, Lucy and Linda, plus Mr. Williams was nice enough to give me a picture with Lucy's autograph on it. They did a lot of things like that, and they really tried to get along with the rest of the staff.

They both used to tell stories about President Johnson and talked about how he could be ruthless at times and then at other times he could be very nice. Mr. Williams told me once how Mr. Johnson bought him some stock in a radio station. But at the same time, Williams said Johnson couldn't understand what it meant to be black, driving across the country and being told that he couldn't get gas or couldn't stay in a motel. Johnson never really understood what that meant, and Williams thought he should because this is such a racist society. Williams said that even when he would tell people that he worked for Lyndon Johnson, well it worked sometimes for some people, but if you're deep down South it didn't carry much weight.

Williams had gray hair and a black mustache. Rumor around work was that he probably dyed it a little bit.

Samuel Wright was a tall, dark-skinned guy, more of a sport or a braggart. He was a sharp dresser and liked the limelight. Sammy passed away around the 1970s. I was delivering a package on Capitol Hill the day I heard about it. The next day I was on an elevator in the Capitol building with this other guy who worked on the Hill; he knew I was a White House messenger, so he asked me if I knew Sammy Wright. I said, "Yes," then I told him that he passed away the day before.

Then he said, "Oh, my God, I guess my money died, too." He had loaned Sammy some money, and apparently Sammy borrowed money from a lot of people to support his flamboyant lifestyle.

I was still on the C.I.A. payroll and detailed to the White House during my first few years there. I was surprised to learn that there were guys at the White House who had been on the job much longer than I—fifteen years—and they were paid less. I was a grade five (a clerk), and these guys were grades two, three, and four (messengers and miscellaneous services). It didn't matter what they did.

There reached a point where that didn't seem fair, so I went to the supervisor, George Parker, about the issues. He said he couldn't do anything about it, but I didn't understand. George Parker was something of an Uncle Tom. He seemed like he was afraid to buck the system. He was much older than I, and he reminded me in a lot of ways of the minister my father had the run-ins with back in Front Royal. Mr. Parker took over for a man named Nash, who had taken ill and had to retire.

The night of October 13,1993 Frank Wills (L) security guard who caught the Watergate burgulars in 1972. Picture with my cousin James Washington Jr. (C) drove from Richmond Virginia to Maryland to attend the fundraiser to witness Frank receiving his Tear Plaque. Yours truly (R)

After seeing that Mr. Parker wasn't going to do anything, I went to William Hopkins, who was executive secretary to the president. Back then I was young, so I guess I approached him with a bit of an attitude, but it really came from not seeing people respected. I guess it came from my experiences growing up and having to deal with the racism and unfairness there. Anyway, I took my paycheck in and laid it on the desk, and I discussed with him the disparities with the way others here were paid. He replied that what I had to say was reasonable and that he would talk to Parker. The fact that Congress had recently passed the 1964 Civil Rights Bill banning discrimination in public accommodations, education, and employment probably played significantly in his consideration.

After a couple of months nothing had happened, so I went back to Mr. Parker for another meeting. I told him there was one guy there who was a grade three and who had a wife and three children and was working two jobs just to make ends meet.

I gave Mr. Parker a deadline to put those promotions through, and I left his office. The meeting on the day after the deadline was very short. I looked at him and said, "Did you or did you not?" He knew what I was talking about and said "No." I did an about face and went back across the hall to Mr. Hopkins and told him about it.

I went out on my daily assignment. When I got back, Mr. Parker came up to me and told me that he was going to put through the promotions. About a month later, some of the guys started getting their promotions. What followed were real job descriptions for every section of the White House—no longer were all the blacks just "messengers and miscellaneous services." Little did I know that at the same time, my friend Pierpoint Mobley who had been promoted to senior personnel specialist was helping Mr. Parker in writing job descriptions and also working on the personnel office's Affirmative Action Plan. Mobley was the first black to hold that position in over fifty years in the personnel office. His placement in this position at that specific time allowed him the opportunity to activate his commitment to help change the status of blacks into reality. By 1970 they switched their policy to where you had to be on the White House payroll to stay there, so I went ahead and switched from working as a person detailed from the C.I.A.

The longer I worked at the White House, the more my perceptions changed about the government. When Malcolm X died in 1965 nobody really talked about it at work because they were more into Martin Luther King. They didn't really understand Malcolm because the media had made him out to be a violent person who would take up arms at any moment. They all wanted to see what King would do because they wanted a safer way, a more nonviolent way to earn their freedom. The death of Medgar Evers, N.A.A.C.P. field secretary and voter registration activist, had more of an effect on me because I had been a member of the N.A.A.C.P. since I was fifteen years old. Others on the job didn't know much about him, except that he had been ambushed at his home in Jackson, Mississippi, on June 12, 1963.

I remember watching King's funeral on television and wishing I could have been there. We couldn't really participate in marches because of our jobs. Nevertheless, I felt that I was a part of this historic event by fulfilling my responsibility to the National Guard protecting the firemen who were providing an important service to our Capital City, Washington, D.C. I did march in the 1963 March on Washington, but that was before the White House job. I remember I had a strange dream the night before King died that my brother John had died; it woke me up in the middle of the night. He had a real effect on me because I had always thought that he was such a great orator, a modern day prophet and someone after whom I wanted to pattern myself.

I liked his nonviolent approach. He would expose the enemy for how evil they were but without fighting back. He appealed to the best in people the way a lot of other leaders did not. When people all over the world saw those dogs being set loose on human beings in Birmingham and Selma and other parts of the South, then heard him urge passive resistance, he elevated the whole Civil Rights Movement to a spiritual level. He was also willing to sacrifice himself by going to jail and standing in the face of angry mobs, and ultimately he paid with his life. Reverend Dr. Martin Luther King, Jr. was assassinated by a sniper April 4, 1968, in Memphis, Tennessee, by segregationist James Earl Ray only a few days after he led a disrupted protest march for striking sanitation workers. The nation mourned and violence erupted in black communities across the nation, resulting in the death of forty-one blacks and five whites.

My mother told me that she got a phone call after King died from some white lady who wouldn't give her name. All my mother heard on the other end of the phone was laughter, then the woman yelled, "We got that black son of a bitch!"

When I saw him in 1963 speaking at the Lincoln Memorial, I couldn't believe he could draw that many people. I was a radio operator for the Guard in 1968. My unit was activated for twelve days on the streets of Washington after King was killed, and I was assigned to protect the firemen. I remember the fire station I was assigned to: New Hampshire and Georgia Avenues. There was a drug store on that corner that burned throughout the night.

After the D.C. government had implemented its 1968 curfew a few days after the King riots had started, I was riding through northeast D.C. on National Guard duty and saw two policemen on H Street talking to a black youngster. He was in handcuffs and they were pretty animated, so we pulled over to see what was happening. They were exchanging words, strong language, and one policeman seemed like he was trying to bait the young man into doing something.

At one point, the officer told the kid he would take the handcuffs off and dared him to run. The kid said he would rather not. He knew he would be shot if he tried to leave. I kept hoping the kid would use some sense and not take the bait because I could see where the policeman was trying to take it. I wanted so badly to say something, but I realized that, because of my own uniform, it was better for me to keep my mouth shut.

They finally arrested the young man, but I never heard what happened to him after that. When Martin Luther King, Jr., was killed, it was hard for me not to feel that the government wasn't involved. I didn't have any proof, but it was just a feeling that wouldn't go away. In 1975 the national press revealed that the F.B.I. and the C.I.A. have frequently conducted intensive spy campaigns including wiretapping, surveillance, and background investigations on prominent black individuals and groups. Among the most aggressively pursued targets were Reverend Dr. Martin Luther King, Jr.; the Black Panthers; and Eartha Kitt, who had been embroiled in a confrontation with Lady Bird Johnson.

I had that same uneasy feeling over the way they stopped Muhammad Ali from boxing because he refused to be drafted into the military because of his opposition to the Vietnam War.

At work we would talk among ourselves about it, and I said I thought Ali would win against the government. A lot of the other guys said he was going to be made an example of because he challenged the government. A lot of them also had gone into the service and felt he should have gone in too, but I looked at it differently. I saw him doing the same thing some of the whites were doing. Remember, at that same time Charles Robb was dating one of President Johnson's daughters, and of course he was in the service, but you knew he wasn't going to get anywhere near the front line.

Dressed in my MP uniform. Picture taken in barracks just before going on guard duty

I figured Ali, being a minister and having religious differences with the war, should have had the right not to go. Besides, being in the Guard I saw a lot of pro athletes who didn't even have to report for our drills. Before the thing with Ali, the athletes would just sign their names on a list, and that would be that.

There was a guy named Pete Rickert in my unit who was a pitcher for the Baltimore Orioles. He was a nice, down-to-earth guy. He told me one day that if it wasn't for Ali, he wouldn't even have to report for the meetings. There was another guy who played for the Redskins, Larry Brown, who also was in the Guard. The National Guard higher-ups decided that the athletes had to start going to reserve meetings out of fear that the press would check into them and sway public opinion to Ali's cause.

The Poor People's Campaign in 1968 brought thousands of African Americans to Washington, D. C., to protest racial discrimination. Under the leadership of Ralph Abernathy, Dr. Martin Luther King's successor as head of the SCLC, the protesters created a temporary encampment, known as "Shantytown" and "Resurrection City," near the Lincoln Memorial. I was at the Poor Peoples' March after King was gone, but I was there in my capacity as a guardsman. I think that was Ralph Abernathy's first march. It was a terrible week. It was raining the whole time, and the protesters' encampments on the Mall were knee deep in mud.

The park police had given the protesters a deadline for getting off the grounds. I remember riding in a jeep near the camps, and I saw policemen stealing typewriters and things like that out of the tents and putting them in the trunks of their own cars. You knew they weren't confiscating items to take back to the station; they were stealing, plain and simple.

That whole era, the 1960s, was kind of confusing. I could understand the protesters, but while I could see it I also was involved on the opposite side. The Guard got called up for a lot of the Vietnam protests. The white guys in our unit were scared, and they would push the blacks to the front line. I spent a lot of time on the front lines. To tell the truth, I never really thought anybody was going to try anything on us, but there was a rumor out there that we should watch our eyes because the protesters were throwing oven cleaner at the troopers. But those protesters didn't mess with us.

I did see one policeman go after a kid holding a VietCong rebels flag, knock him to the ground, and arrested him.

I was pretty much living on my own during my days in the White House. Almost every Sunday I went to church at Tenth Street Baptist Church. I would go to movies and go on a date or two. But working for the C.I.A., my main focus was keeping my nose clean because I knew they would ask questions about where I went, what night clubs or bars I'd been to, and all of that. I really didn't go in for that much, but I would go to cabarets held in the basements of the Catholic churches, where social groups would rent out the halls and you could bring your own liquor. Until my first marriage in 1968, I had to cook for myself too—something I didn't have to do much on the farm with two sisters in the house. Life for me was pretty bland.

It was Reverend Thomas J. Jennings, from the Tenth Street Baptist Church, who told me in 1966 about a co-op on O Street in southwest D.C. What I liked about it was that it was in a nice neighborhood and, I later learned, that I lived around the corner from where Hubert Humphrey lived. Of course, he didn't live exactly in the same kind of place I did; you had rich folks on one side and the poor folks on the other.

The place was a little one-bedroom condo that the government had rehabilitated, and it was mine. I had lived with somebody else my whole life, even in Washington, until my new wife moved in with me in the exclusive southwest section of Washington, D.C. The location was nice, and it felt like progress.

Senator Robert Kennedy was assassinated in 1968 in Los Angeles, California, after he won the California Democratic primary. Coretta Scott King joined Kennedy's widow, Ethel, on the plane that returned Kennedy's body to New York. There were no riots after Bobby Kennedy's death, but we were dispatched again to line the funeral procession route. That year we also knew that President Johnson was not going to run for re-election and that it was going to come down to my neighbor, Hubert Humphrey, and Richard Nixon. I hate to say it, but I just didn't like Nixon. I had heard about his nickname, "Tricky Dick," and I heard he had done a number on this lady he was running against in California called the "Pink Pages." He had put out all of this dirt on her, and from what we heard, a lot of it wasn't true. He seemed dishonest, and I really didn't want him to win the election over Humphrey.

After Nixon won, there was a different kind of White House from what we had with Johnson. I remember our first Christmas party was a very stuffy candlelight affair. All we did was stroll through the East Wing and shake his and Pat's hands, and that was it. There was a black chef named John Ficklin from Hume, Virginia, who had grown up with my mother. He made eggnog with a secret ingredient which he did not reveal until after his retirement. It was great eggnog. Mr. Ficklin also had been the chef for Johnson's Christmas parties, which were a lot more fun. There was music and dancing and plenty of good food.

Johnson used to throw old Western-style barbecues and bring his own cooks up from Texas to cook the beef ribs. Except for the Christmas parties, we were allowed to bring our families, and even Johnson himself was easier to talk to. Before he left office in 1969, he posed for a photograph with all of the messengers. I got each of them to sign it, but I couldn't get the president's autograph on it because he was busy moving out of the White House and back to Texas.

When it came time for President Nixon's reelection and news of the Watergate break-in came out, I figured he was guilty of something. It was probably my dislike for him that fueled my suspicions.

Every now and then I would see some of his aides coming and going, but for the most part, they worked in the Executive Office Building. Inside the White House, the security is like it is on the outside. If you saw Nixon coming down the hallway, he was always flanked by two security guards, and he would walk by and not even acknowledge you the way Johnson would.

I got to meet a lot of important policy makers during my time there, but for the most part I just went to their offices, dropped off my packages, and left. James Brown came through there one time, and we rode up on the same elevator in the Executive Office Building. I didn't say much to him except, "Hello." Another time I saw Sammy Davis, Jr., come to visit, and to tell you the truth, I lost a little respect for both of them for coming to see Nixon. You knew they were both coming there for something, and Sammy was a registered Republican and had the nerve to go hugging on Nixon. We always figured he came looking for some kind of presidential appointment. He was widely criticized among blacks and liberal whites for endorsing President Nixon's policies and for allowing nationwide distribution of the photograph showing him hugging President Nixon.

Looking back, I feel pretty much the same way. I admired Sammy as an artist, but I still can't respect how he lowered and demeaned himself in front of Nixon. It still embarrasses me. James Brown didn't lower himself before Nixon the way Sammy did, which softened my view of him. But in later years, he lost my respect when he went around shooting a gun at his wife and leading police on a high-speed chase before going to jail. Now that he is out of jail, I hope his life will one day be as positive as his music.

As President Nixon's reelection campaign swung into full gear, those of us in the messenger force began delivering more and more brown overstuffed envelopes that were different from what we were used to delivering. We were never told about the contents, but that didn't seem so unusual since we often were not informed about the contents of any cargo. I remember, though, that we all had our suspicions about what was inside. Many of us joked that it was probably slush money, but we didn't know for certain.

Several times I would walk packages back and forth from the White House to the Executive Office Building and to the president's reelection headquarters about a block away. Often I was held around until five o'clock or a little later by Mr. James Smoot, supervisor of the Executive Office Building's mailroom, and was told to drop off one of these envelopes on my way home. He kept the envelopes in his desk and watched them like a hawk and would only say that it was important that they got delivered as quickly as possible.

A friend and I waiting in line to visit the eternal flame grave of our assassinated President John F. Kennedy.

Posing in the entrance of then my work place the west wing to the White House with Mrs. Goode working in the background

Chapter Four
Treat Everyone Right

In 1986, I wrote a letter to South African President P.W. Botha after I had read in the newspaper about the township of Soweto and how black people were being treated there. I wanted to explain to him my true feelings, and I wanted to ask him how he would feel if someone treated him that way because of his color. What surprised me is that he actually wrote back.

Basically, all he said was that they were trying to make conditions better and that they had been working with Archbishop Desmond Tutu. With the letter, they sent three copied pages, reports about their efforts. Maybe they just wanted to let me know that they weren't such bad people.

I'm not sure exactly why I chose that time to write. I think it was because of what I saw about Soweto, about the killings, and I hated to see people suffering for no good reason. I realize that my little letter didn't alter the course of history or anything, but doing so gave me a special feeling four years later when I watched Nelson Mandela being released from prison after all those years.

Mandela never yielded during the twenty-seven years he spent behind bars; South Africa's racism never broke him. Instead, he took it and told his people to keep fighting, whatever the cost, rather than succumb to the wishes of their enemies. South Africa imprisoned Mandela's body but not his mind; now he's their president. His struggle in South Africa made it possible for me to look back on going to high school in Front Royal, Virginia, and know that the same spirit moved inside the two of us.

Maybe it's no coincidence that I finally was able to walk from my own personal prison: returning to Warren County High School for the first time since graduation. Just as Mandela was locked away physically from the world until 1990, I was locked away emotionally from Warren County and what it had meant to me.

In 1989 I went back to the school with my sister and three classmates to take part in a short news feature about our experiences there as the first black students. After graduation in 1961, I had vowed never to return, wanting to dismiss the whole thing as nothing more than a bad memory. But as we stood at the bottom of what once had seemed like the world's steepest hill, looking up at the school, a sense of satisfaction came over me. I was looking at my alma mater, and for the first time it felt like my alma mater.

Gone were the screaming protesters hurling racial epithets in my direction. Gone was the fat white woman, blushing beet red and seething at me for desecrating her sacred institution; shouting that she would "kill all of you niggers."

A lot of the ideas I always had held deep inside about how we should treat one another began coming together for me then. What had started in high school all those years ago—and continued into my years with the White House and into everything I did—started making sense. But it was a spark from one incident that shined a light too bright to ignore: the beating of black motorist Rodney King by Los Angeles police in 1991 and the "not guilty" verdict handed down a year later by an all-white jury.

I was outraged like everyone else to see that, even with the videotaped evidence of those officers beating him, those men were acquitted. I decided to write my first letter to the editor of the *Capital*, a newspaper in Annapolis, Maryland. I made a suggestion that we change the name of the White House to the "LEADER" House, standing for Lead Every American to Denounce Everywhere Racism. I then suggested that we elect a president who is opposed to the racist element in this country, a president who does not represent the rich and powerful while totally ignoring the minority population and their issues.

We needed somebody with Kennedy's compassion, Johnson's follow-through, without Nixon's cold-hearted indifference, I thought. That was the first time I recommended the TEAR process—Treat Every American Right—and started my organization of the same name. After that, I received about fifty phone calls from people saying that what I wrote was right on time. Then my neighbor came by and asked me to autograph a copy of the article that he had photocopied on "good quality paper." He said he wanted to put it in a frame and up on his wall.

He kept repeating, "Treat every American right; treat every American right." I starting thinking then that maybe this really was a good idea. I sat in my kitchen and began to sketch out an idea. I drew two faces—one black and one white, and both facing

Treat Every American Right multi-cultural humanitarian image message.
Courtesy of the Northern Virginia Daily newspaper

the American flag—and wrote the words underneath. I'm no artist, so I found one who suggested putting ragged edges on the flag and then putting the images on T-shirts and posters.

When I went down to the patent office to get my copyright, the man at the desk saw my design and bought two on the spot. But it really wasn't just about marketing the shirts and posters; it was about a message. I thought about Frank Grier, an innocent man wrongly accused in 1961. His only real crime was graduating from Warren County High School, and he caught hell for it.

And I thought about Rodney King and how if that jury had done the right thing there would not have been any rioting in Los Angeles and across the country. All of that damage could have been avoided, and they would not have needed that second trial. If nothing else, if we "treated everyone right" in that case, it would have been a lot less costly in terms of lives and property.

In 1993 I read in *Jet* magazine that Frank Wills, the man who found the tape on the door at the Watergate Office Building, was having a hard time. His discovery led to the arrest of burglars inside Democratic Committee headquarters and eventually to Nixon's resignation. Nowadays Frank has been reduced to near nothing. He moved from Washington to his home town of North Augusta, South Carolina, in 1990 to care for his mother, who had been felled by a stroke. After she passed away, he didn't have the money to bury her, so he had to donate her body to medical research. He was washing his clothes out of a bucket and was just barely getting by when I called him and said I wanted to have a fund-raiser in his honor.

In many ways, putting on our fund-raiser for Frank represented an attempt to put my money where my mouth was. I remembered Frank Wills from the Watergate era. Sometimes I would deliver packages over to the Democratic Committee headquarters and while we weren't friends or anything I knew who he was. When I told him I wanted to do a fund-raiser for him, he consented and came up from South Carolina.

Frank Wills was a small-built man who didn't look much different than when I saw him on the job. He looked surprisingly youthful for a man in his forties. He stayed in my home for the five days he was in town and we spent some time talking and sharing memories. He said he had tried to get several jobs after Watergate but had no success. He even went to Howard University but was told that they could not hire him because the school might lose its federal money if he was on the payroll.

He felt like he hadn't been treated properly while all of the burglars and conspirators got rich writing books, making speeches, and getting radio shows. When the Democratic National Committee sent him a plaque, he told them that was all fine and good but he "couldn't eat no plaque." He was bitter, and it was hard for him to understand how he had gone from a hero to somebody no one wanted around.

People could relate to Frank, too, because here was a man who had just done his job and he was punished for it while the criminals made millions. Frank was an easily understandable symbol for my slogan, "Treat Every American Right," because he just did his job while the people with the capital and money could take advantage by breaking the law. I saw something wrong about that. I felt some kinship for him because we both had some connection to Watergate, though nobody will ever write much about either of us. I always thought of him over the years, and it seemed like God was talking to me and telling me I should do something for this man.

Prior to Frank coming to town, I did an interview with an Annapolis television station. I told the host that a lot of people had forgotten about Frank and the role he played in Watergate. I talked about the time I met a young black attorney who had always thought that Frank was a white man.

Frank had this hope that he would be treated at least as good as the burglars and that he would get the interviews, the book deals, and the money that came with it. He figured this would be his big break, but he was just an ordinary person. He didn't have the education, or much family support—his mother was very ill. He never spoke about his father, and there were no brothers and sisters, no real close aunts and uncles. It was sort of like he was all alone in the world. A few people tried to help him early on, including activist Dick Gregory, who was a 1968 presidential candidate; *Roots* author Alex Haley; and columnist William Raspberry. Dick Gregory had given Frank a job working for Gregory's diet centers in the Bahamas and Florida, and he was one of the few people who made an effort to keep Frank's name in the public consciousness, but it just never worked out for Frank.

I had planned an agenda for Frank's visit. After picking him up from Baltimore/Washington International Airport, we had dinner. The next morning I took him to two different Sunday morning church services at Greater Mt. Nebo AME Church in Upper Marlboro, Maryland, and then at my church—Asbury Broadneck United Methodist Church in Annapolis. When it came time for visitors to stand, he did so and was greeted warmly by the congregations.

Katherine Chase, an usher at Greater Mt. Nebo A.M.E. Church, was quite taken with Frank and invited him and me to her house for dinner later in that week. She treated us to a down-home country-style meal with fried fish, collard greens, pinto beans, mashed potatoes, corn bread, and a yellow cake with vanilla icing for dessert. Sister Katherine, as I called her, thought Frank was kind of handsome and flirted with him throughout the meal. She invited him to look her up if he ever came back to town.

Frank also was invited to a fund-raiser in Annapolis for Baltimore Mayor Kurt Schmoke. Another stop was Annapolis High School, where he spoke to the Concerned Black Male Students group, which Orlie Reid started and with which I was a volunteer counselor to troubled students.

We appeared on two talk shows, including WOL in Washington, where Gregory was the host. One television station sent a news crew to my house to interview Frank, and a reporter from the *Baltimore Sun* also stopped by. Frank was a natural with the press, and he didn't really mind talking to them because he had done it so many times. He had his story of that night down, with no details left out. But maybe Frank expected too much, expected that the world owed him more because he had blown the cover on the Nixon White House.

The night of the fund-raiser, we had the Inspiration Choir from the Asbury Broadneck United Methodist Church of Annapolis, the church I had been a member of for nine years. The choir sang one song that seemed particularly appropriate for the night—"Give Somebody Hope Today." Vera Thompson, who was a local radio personality, was our emcee, Alderman Carl Snowden was the speaker, and there were several television cameras and newspapers there. We had helped Frank put together his speech. After he spoke, my sister Patricia gave him the TEAR plaque. It went very well.

We raised about seven-hundred-fifty dollars that we could give to Frank, and he appreciated it. I think it made him feel good to know that someone cared about him. I think we both thought that the attention maybe would lead to something big for him.

The day after the event, Frank and an old friend went to the Duke Ellington School for the Arts in Washington, where he received a certificate. That same day, Frank Simon, a columnist from the *Sun* called and asked how much we had given him, and when I told him, he told us we were crazy to try to help Frank and that he was just a cheap hustler who had taken advantage of us.

Note: (CBM) Concerned Black Males of Annapolis, Md. CBM student deligation members relaxing after taking part in a martial arts demonstration at the Children's Palace, Beijing, China.

In his editorial critique of Frank, Simon talked about Frank's lack of education and wrote,

> The Watergate criminals who did profit not only had
> college educations, but lifetimes of powerful contacts in
> business, government and the media. Wills had none of
> that. He did gain celebrity status, but instead of trying
> to use it to finance an education or get into a steady job,
> he seems to have expected some large lump sum reward.
> And when he didn't get one, he turned into a professional
> victim, repeating his tale of woe year after year.

I didn't feel that way at all. To tell the truth I wanted to pass a lesson on to the kids that when you see a brother who has been knocked on the ground, try to reach down and pick him up. We figured that we could provide a spark that would get him back on his feet.

The last I heard was that Frank was losing his home and that things had gotten worse. I tried to call him in 1995, and he did call back and left a message, but when I tried to call him again the phone had been disconnected. I found another number for him, but all I got was a voice-mail message. I left a message for him to call me but I never heard from him again.

Looking at Frank's life, it's almost easy to believe that respect is something that doesn't apply if you are a black man. I thought about that later as I sat in a restaurant eating eggs and bacon. I couldn't help but think about Frank and how important it was to get my message to treat everyone right to as many people as possible.

I wasn't paying much attention to the waiter, who slammed my breakfast down in front of me and quickly vanished. No matter; I was in too much of a hurry to comment about it because I only had time enough to eat and run before my ten o'clock appointment. I paid my bill and headed on my way.

I didn't think much about the half-dozen black men who entered the restaurant as I was leaving. All were well-dressed, wearing dark suits, and were very polite. I spoke to the first one as he entered; he nodded back. About two days later I learned that they were White House Secret Service men—and that the Denny's Restaurant we had both eaten at had refused them service.

Being a former White House employee myself, I felt an attachment to the men. It reminded me of what we tell our children sometimes, that no matter how much you do in life, you are still judged on what you look like. It is a truth shared by all black men, no matter how much they achieve in this country; it is unspoken, yet always there. You want to tell yourself that another degree, a great job, more money, fame, or something else will wipe the stain away and allow you to feel as a human rather than as the evil in somebody else's eyes.

When I heard the black agents were going to appear in Baltimore on Kweisi Mfume's talk show, *The Bottom Line,* I went down there to sit in the audience. When I spoke with them after the show, I told them how I had once worked at the White House, that I had seen them enter Denny's that morning, and how much I sympathized with what they had gone through.

I wished them well with their lawsuit—which became a class-action suit that they eventually won—and told them about my TEAR idea. We left each other agreeing that treating people with just a little respect was the way we all should go. I later joined in the Denny's protest march.

Another one of my designed multi-cultural humanitarian image messages. Title: Turn Everyone in the world Against Racism.

Chapter Five
The Great Wall

There are times when I still wonder how we pulled off going to China. I was chairman of the local N.A.A.C.P.'s education committee when I met Orlie Reid, a child psychotherapist who was in charge of something called the Education Equity Committee. I attended their Thursday night meetings, and I soon learned about a project he was trying to put together at Annapolis High School, called Concerned Black Males. Most of the kids he dealt with weren't much interested in education. They spent more time cracking heads than they did cracking the books, and Orlie counseled the students on how to behave.

I agreed to join his team at the school. We'd meet every Tuesday morning to decide what we would do with the kids on Wednesday. We would show up at the school early, about seven o'clock, so that the first thing the kids would see was this group of black men. We would stand in the hallway as they walked in, and if we saw the kids walking in with their pants pulled down too low or with caps on their heads, we would call them aside and get them to look presentable.

There also was a conference room at the school where we would meet with students referred to us by the school counselor. I'll never forget the look on this one young man's face when he walked in and saw seven professional black men waiting for him. We'd let him know that we were there to help, then we would go over whatever it was he had done. The young man would give his side of the story, and we would give him advice on how to respond. The young man would promise not to do it again, and most times we would not have much trouble with him.

Summer of 1995 standing on the Great Wall of China with Chinese tourist.

There was one young kid who got kicked off the basketball team because of his behavior. He had been fighting and had a reputation as a roughneck. He was a big kid, and he looked a lot older than high-school age, but what struck me about him was how humble he was in front of us. Maybe it was the sight of all of us older men in the room.

When we asked him what had happened, he told us some guy had been messing with him and that he wasn't gonna let the guy get away with it. We told him that he needed to learn some restraint because there were going to be a lot of situations in life that would be a lot tougher than that. After we talked to him and got him to get it together, Orlie got him reinstated on the team, and he even graduated.

To us, these were young men headed for trouble. A lot of them came from one-parent homes and, for the most part, they were good kids who had just made some bad choices. They didn't understand what an education could do or that the teachers in there with them had gotten theirs already. They had jobs, and if they wanted to get a job too, they were going to have to be a lot more serious.

Some of them reminded me of the hardheads with whom I had grown up with. A few of them ended up in reform school—and it looked like these young ones would go the same way.

During our second year with the program, we decided to train student leaders who could help handle disputes. Since the leaders were there every day, they would represent the Concerned Black Males and serve as an example. They got to be leaders by making a significant change in their own attitudes and signing an oath to adhere to certain rules. As long as they conducted themselves in a proper way, and attended the meetings we held, they would remain in the group. When it came time to chose the group that we would take to China, we picked them from this group.

Orlie Reid was the one who made the China trip possible. He had been to China the year before, 1994. He had been chosen by a professional group, the Citizen Ambassador program of people to people international. Mr. Reid, a Psychotherapist, was one of thirty-four professionals worldwide for the exchange program to the People's Republic of China. When he came back, Orlie decided that he wanted to take black students over there to give them a sense of another culture, so he connected with a group called the China Association for Science and Technology (C.A.S.T.), which was part of the China International Conference Center for Science and Technology, which helped him arrange the trip.

There were thirteen kids and five adults. We met at Orlie's office on July 25. We headed out from National Airport, and even then you could hear the excitement with the young men. For many of them it was their first time on an airplane. We stopped in Chicago at O'Hare Airport, to change planes to board the China Eastern Airlines and some of the boys decided to call home to check in. I guess some of them were homesick after just a few short hours.

One young guy finished up his call, and he was so excited that he left his wallet at the phone. A chaperone went back with him, but of course the wallet was gone. Luckily his money wasn't in the wallet.

From Chicago we flew five hours to Seattle and then ten hours to Beijing. There wasn't a whole lot to do on the way over except sleep, eat a lot, and watch a few movies—mostly about the Chinese. I got a lot of sleep. A few of us talked about what to expect when we got there, what we would see.

The fact that I was going to China hit me pretty early on. Actually it really hit me in the morning as I got ready to leave home. I had only been married ten days, and here I was going halfway around the world without my wife. I got married for the second time on July 15, went on the honeymoon on the 17th, got back on the 23rd, and started packing to take off right away. Believe me, she was very understanding.

When we arrived in Beijing, we knew immediately that we had come to a different kind of place. You see all of these people who are speaking words you don't know, and you try to read signs that are in Chinese, but since an interpreter met us when we landed, we didn't really have to worry much about those kinds of things. She stood in the terminal holding a little C.A.S.T. flag.

The bus was very small and cramped. It had fold-down seats that went between the fixed regular seats, but it did have air conditioning. The driver spoke a little English, and he was funny. Our tour guide introduced him as Jack, but I'm not sure that was his real name. The side roads were a lot narrower than roads in the United States, but the main highways were pretty much like our own. There wasn't a whole lot of traffic outside the city, but once you got into the city, there were people riding bicycles everywhere you looked.

On the first night, the hosts threw a party for us that included Chinese youngsters. Our kids had to participate in the opening ceremonies, as did the young people from China. Their kids had banjos, and they sang a few "American" songs—you know, to make us feel welcome. Our boys did a rap tune; really it was a song from that Joe Clark movie, *Lean on Me*. They had a second rap that had something to do with their high school, and they were "whooping" and barking.

There was a young girl there who was very tall, and she was introduced to Reggie Snowden, who was one of our young guys. It seemed that from the very first the two of them hit it off, and every time an event or something came up she would come over and sit with him. Reggie had himself a girlfriend.

We stayed at the Zi Yu Hotel. The beds were small, and the showers had a spray nozzle. We had been instructed not to drink the water, but there was a thermos of hot water in each room to be used for brushing teeth, and bottled water was available.

On the street in Beijing, there were vegetable stands and food markets on every corner. You got used to seeing side streets and alleys packed with open-air markets and jammed with people moving hurriedly about. Everything was written in Chinese, but there was an occasional Coca-Cola sign to be seen, and there was a McDonald's and a Kentucky Fried Chicken in town—something American.

We ate at a different restaurant every night. One had a terrarium with snakes in it and another with frogs in it. Every table had a Lazy Susan where the waiter set the food, and the biggest challenge was trying to use chopsticks. There were no forks. We preferred the wooden sticks because they were less slippery than the plastic ones.

Every time a new dish was brought to our table we made a point to ask what it was.

"Is it chicken or beef or pork?" somebody would ask the guide, wanting to make sure we weren't getting served a snake. One day we did get frog legs, but they were pretty small. We drank a lot of green tea, though some of the restaurants served Coke and Sprite.

After eating we would head out for some activity or another, which was good because there was nothing to watch on television and what few shows did come on were in Chinese anyway.

We had a full schedule. We would get up early each morning and eat an "American" breakfast with something that looked like French toast with jelly that looked like apple butter, some tea, eggs—I guess they thought everybody in America ate their eggs sunny-side up because that's the way we got them. There was no sausage, no bacon, no meat of any kind. Occasionally, we were served round pieces of meat about the size of a fifty-cent coin that resembled bologna but tasted more like liverwurst.

We usually would visit schools where we would have cultural exchanges with the students. The Chinese kids would put on a show for us, almost always in English because each school had English teachers and the kids were eager to show us what they knew. They would then present us with gifts, and then they would ask us questions about America. They would usually ask the men if we had any kids and ask us all how we liked their country, how the weather was different. The English teachers told us that they always wanted to come to America.

Two groups challenged our kids to games of basketball, and sad to say our boys lost both times! What happened was the challenge was made to play this game the following day. Our boys said, "Okay, no problem," then went back to the hotel that night and talked about how many slam dunks they were going to get.

Game time came, and all of these tall Chinese guys walked out onto the court, and we said, "These guys don't go to this school, do they?" They didn't. Somebody went out into the community and rounded up the biggest guys they could find. The other problem was that the game was outside on dirt. Now the Chinese guys would pass the ball from spot to spot, but our guys started dribbling the ball, wanting to play some one-on-one; next thing you know the ball has gotten away from them.

They beat us, and Orlie pulled them aside afterwards and told them, "You guys beat yourselves today. You see how those guys passed?"

The next week we played another group, and we figured the guys had learned from the first experience. The score was close because our guys came out passing. But then they started dribbling again, and the same thing happened—these big tall Chinese guys came out and passed, and our guys tried to be like Mike. They lost again.

Our boys were hardheaded like that, figuring that just because they walked out on the court they always were going to win. We used the defeats to teach them lessons about teamwork and about being prepared for anything, but some people had to be shown.

We got up real early this one day and went to the park. There were a lot of senior citizens exercising in the park, and we were told they did this every morning. When we got there, there was a man going through a wrestling match with a smaller guy, and he was throwing him all over the place. Orlie's son, Orlie, Jr., had taken karate, and he thought he was pretty good, so Orlie urged the boy to wrestle.

The kid got up there with this old man, and the elder flipped him over quick. Orlie, Sr. got embarrassed then.

"Why don't you do what they taught you?" he pleaded to his son. "Always defend yourself. You can't let him do that to you."

So one of the adult men, Jim Stroud, came out and wrestled the old guy, and he held his own with him, and neither one of them got thrown. Jim was a big man, and what he did was to play it real smart. By the time they were done, Orlie had convinced his son to give it another try. This time, he was more careful, and they sparred around until the old man said he'd had enough and ended the match.

Of course Orlie went on about how his son could have thrown the old guy if he'd wanted to but he didn't want to embarrass the guy in his own country. But the old one had proven his point.

As we walked around to the various landmarks we drew crowds. People would gather to watch us, and our guys were so big—and we were all black—that people thought we were a basketball team. One person would break the ice and ask one of the students to take a picture with her, then we would have groups of people coming around waiting to get their pictures taken. It was like we were celebrities. That would go on for a long while.

The people were nice, and though we couldn't speak Chinese we managed to communicate in some ways. On one trip we were divided into several groups which we were invited to dinner with some Chinese students and their families. My group walked with a female student to her house and met her mother and father, a marketing representative for a beer company. An English-speaking teacher accompanied us.

As the mother prepared dinner, the father brought out a few small cans of beer from its storage place under the bed, opened them, and then set them on the dinner table in front of me and the boys. I kept trying to tell him I didn't want any beer and that the boys shouldn't have any, but the boys were no help as they tried to boldly reassure me that they could handle it. Our host looked at me and insisted, "Ah, it's okay." So I let them drink one beer.

The menu consisted of cut-up chicken, rice, dumplings, sweet and sour pork, hot bread, and a couple of dishes I did not recognize. She was an excellent cook, and you could tell this by looking at her husband, who was a big man. I don't know whether the weight came from the food or the beer. He drank three beers for lunch and offered us more too, but we refused.

The apartment was fairly small, like most of the apartments we saw; I think it only had three rooms in it. The mother encouraged us to eat, and after dinner they showed us a scrapbook and shared some of their lives with us, and they commented on how much the U.S. seemed to have compared to what they had in China.

At the end of dinner, the father offered to send a limousine to shuttle us back to his daughter's school. We were surprised to see a large Toyota Maxima, jet black, parked on the side of the building. It was the largest car we saw during our stay in China.

I remember being struck by how plain some parts of the city looked. Almost everything was gray concrete, no tiles, wood, or fancy facades.

Our tour guide's name was Marjing Ma. She wasn't more than twenty or twenty-one. She was real familiar with the United States, though she had never been here and probably never would come. What we found out is that in China you have to go through a lot to come to the U.S. Marjing said it takes a long time for the process to work, and you have to have a lot of money, and you have to get permission from the government.

Marjing would tell jokes sometimes, and she told us about groups that had come before. She looked out for us, too. After about three or four days of Chinese food, the kids wanted McDonald's. We were supposed to go to this other restaurant, where the main course was dumplings, but nobody wanted to go. So she made arrangements for us to go to a Kentucky Fried Chicken instead. She explained a lot to us and made us feel welcome there.

One thing we learned right away was how much it cost to call home from China. In the hotel room, if you used the right codes, you could hook up with AT & T and call back to the United States. And that wasn't bad. Later, when we went to Xi'an, it was different. You couldn't call back from your room, you had to call from the lobby. The way it worked was that someone at the front desk watched you make the call, and when you got done you had to pay right there.

I went down one time and made a call to my wife, and when I got done they said I had been on for seventeen minutes and that I owed three hundred and some in Chinese money— eighty dollars in American money. Another, a young guy, was on the phone, so I went over to warn him. By the time he was done he owed one hundred twenty-five dollars for thirty minutes. After that the word spread like wildfire, and nobody called for the rest of the trip—or at least not until we got back to Beijing.

The very first day we went to Tiananmen Square, where the students protested against the government and where many of them had lost their lives. The sight reminded me of the Vietnam and civil rights protests I saw in America. I reflected back to Front Royal, walking the gauntlet in search of an education.

A half-dozen soldiers were posted there, statue-like, guarding the grounds. At one end of the square was a large red building. On it, about halfway up, was a larger than life painting of Mao Tse Tung, which seemed to tower over the entire square. His hollow eyes followed us wherever we went.

We went to the Forbidden City and the Great Wall, and to our credit, we only lost one person. We had gone to the Emperor's Summer Palace and toured the different buildings all over the site. When it came time to leave, we realized we were missing someone. Marjing went looking but couldn't find him, so we drove around the outside of the palace to the second gate and looked for him. He had already left his passport on the bus, which worried us, and this time it wasn't one of the kids but one of the adults.

He had gotten separated during the tour; without his passport we feared he would be picked up by the police, and since he spoke no Chinese, we might not be able to find him quickly. We finally did find him right around closing time, but we were so late we had to skip an opera we were supposed to see that night because there was no time to get there.

The Great Wall was something special. When you approach the base of the Wall itself, there's this little area where you park. Everywhere we looked there were people selling souvenirs. You could either walk up to the Wall or take one of these little cabs up to it.

The Wall has cutouts for the guns on one side, while the other was just straight across; I guess they didn't have to worry about their backs. It's just a long, concrete wall. Now I didn't try to walk the whole thing, but the kids did it easily. What struck me more about the whole scene was the surrounding area, with green mountains and valleys. Coming from a part of the United States where we have a lot of hills—Skyline Drive, Luray Caverns—the sight reminded me of home. You could see for miles on a normal day, but the day we went was a little cloudy. Still, it was breathtaking.

In the Forbidden City we learned about the lives of the people who lived there. I was surprised to hear about how much the women there went through—the emperor's wives. Seems like they just gave up their lives to serve one man. There was another well-known spot where one of the emperors was buried with an army of sculpted soldiers. The theory was that these men would guard the emperor forever, even after death.

The kids were fascinated by what they saw. I don't think any of them had ever left their country before, and you could tell that the sights they saw and the people they met were having an effect on them. Every morning during breakfast we would have a prayer and discuss what we had seen the day before. A couple of days before the end, one young man suggested that we stand holding hands in a circle, and another suggested that each one of us should offer up a prayer.

One young man, J.R. Alexander, had lost his mother a few years ago. He thanked God that he had been able to make the trip, then he said that he wished that his mother could have been alive to see it. I could see the tears running down his face as he spoke. It touched me, and it felt like it touched the others.

We saw a great many things during our stay there. We saw hospitals, museums, schools, government offices, and the palaces. We had a full scope of the country.

On the night before we went home, the host had a dinner for us. They served us a Peking duck, which we were told was a very high honor. They rolled the duck into the room and carved it in front of us. We were told that it was best to eat a little of the skin with the meat for the best effect. Several people made speeches and thanked us for visiting and said they hoped the visits would become a regular event.

As for the boys, after seventeen days they were ready to get back home and see their families.

CBM members visit a Middle School In Xi'an, China. L/R: James Stroud, James Kilby, Orlie W. Reid, Dr. Jean Creek, and Marie Bowers.

After we returned, I saw a couple of the young men. I was at a picnic when I saw one in particular. He came up to me, and we talked about general things about the trip. He said he enjoyed it, but he also enjoyed being back home. The one thing he remembered most, though, was not all of the monuments or great buildings.

He remember this day when we were driving across the farm country. Marjing was still with us, but there was a young man with her who ran this part of the tour and who know about the area. He suggested that we stop at this old farmer's house. Winters there can be just as harsh as the worst we have here.

We went into the man's home, and it was made of little more than straw and clay. There were no walls, just pieces of tin laying on the roof with blocks of cement holding them in place. The old man had this bowl of food, and it looked like it had green peppers with some seasoning. He stopped eating and looked to us. "Would you like to have something to eat," he asked, through the interpreter. We said, "No, thank you."

He took us around and showed us how he lived as though he was proud. His bed was nothing but a couple of pieces of wood with one blanket and no pillow. Then he showed us his daughters' room and the kitchen. In the kitchen was a piece of metal resting on top of a hole in the ground. We were told that this was his stove. He took us outside and showed us his goats and other animals, then he showed us where he stored his food. It wasn't anything but a hole in the ground covered by straw.

This man didn't have anything, but here he was offering us something from his table. He had manners. Can you imagine living that way here?

This young man touched on that as he talked with me at the picnic. "That's amazing," he kept saying to me. "I don't know how he did it."

Epilogue

When I was going through the trials at Warren County High School, I didn't always understand why that was important—to me or those in my community.

In 1995 the Warren County School Board decided on a name for a new elementary school. There were more than twenty names suggested. One woman stood up and said they should name the school for Valerie Smelser, a twelve-year-old white girl who died as a result of child abuse. The woman said she could see Valerie's grave from her kitchen table. Another person wanted to have the school named for an old friend, a white man who once had donated land in Front Royal as a park.

To the Board's credit, they named the school after Hilda Barbour, a black woman who had taught school in Front Royal for forty years.

Of course, I wanted them to name the school after my father since he was the one who started the integration movement. He made a historical contribution, one that the town of Front Royal has never acknowledged. My father had the courage of his convictions, and if he was a white man he would have been honored for it.

In many ways, the 1990s are no different than the 1950s in terms of Front Royal's racial attitudes.

Upon my return thirty-four years after graduating from Warren County High School, I found the word "Blackie" scrawled graffiti-style on the corner of the school. Ku Klux Klan literature was distributed within the community, and the once thriving center of black activity where I socialized as a teen had been visibly neglected to the point of ruin.

In 1996 I called a newspaper to see if they would do a story on the thirty-fifth anniversary of Frank's and my graduation but was met with skepticism from the local press that deemed the anniversary not news-worthy. Just as black people were ignored in the past, we are in many ways still ignored when we try to celebrate the positive. Returning as quickly as I had departed to a town once known as Helltown, with signs of racism still evident, it seems I have come full circle. I have concluded that changing racial attitudes and behaviors will continue to be an uphill battle—a forever fight.

Even today's headlines, with news reports about black churches being burned to the ground, mirror what blacks faced when I was a child. Back then the arsonists were angry about the civil rights movement; today it's affirmative action. An Associated Press article recently reported that race was the motivation in approximately 61 percent of hate crimes in the United States in 1995. Another hot headline which demonstrates the state of race relations is the Texaco class-action suit brought on behalf of 1,500 black employees who were allegedly denied promotions because of race. Tapes of executive meetings revealed demeaning comments made in reference to blacks and discussions to destroy documents related to a race-discrimination suit.

Maybe that's why I try to speak out; I like to see people treated well. I'm not a trouble maker or a revolutionary, just somebody who cares.

In some ways I'm still just a farm boy from Virginia who helped integrate the public schools in my home state; who was lucky enough to have worked in the White House; who saw the civil rights and anti-Vietnam movements in a way different from other folks; who went to China and met people who, it turned out, weren't that much different from me. I'm not bitter about the way my life has gone; in fact I'm somewhat satisfied.

One recognition that I am particularly proud of is the Dallas G. Pace, Sr. Humanitarian Award from the Anne Arundel County Human Realations Commission. That award, presented at the thirteenth Annual Dr. Martin Luther King, Jr. Memorial Breakfast, will always have a special, everlasting effect on me. Upon returning to my seat beside Adrian Wiseman, director of human relations, I listened to him say that my name would be inscribed on a large plaque with past recipients and hung in the County Government Building *forever*. Located at 44 Calvert Street in Annapolis, Maryland, the Arundel Center is only two blocks from the memorial of the late Supreme Court Justice Thurgood Marshall at the Annapolis State Complex. This is the same site where I witnessed the swearing in of Maryland Governor Parris Glendening just two years ago. This closeness to Thurgood Marshall's memorial seems more than coincidental since I consider him to be the architect of the school integration movement in this country in which I participated and of which I am a direct beneficiary.

Now I want to share what I have learned with others.

It is very important for children to have that proper guidance in life. It builds a strong character, and with that you can survive and overcome a lot of things. There is always a way around certain obstacles if you are determined and have goals for your life just like you would have a goal for your business. What I learned is that the decisions you make when you are young affect what you do when you get older. I always worked hard, and I have tried to instill in my children what my parents instilled in me. I know some people think these things are corny or something, but without those things in your life you won't get far as a person.

I was always taught that if you work you can put a roof over your head, and if you can put a roof over your head you can eat healthy, and if you can eat healthy you can keep working, and as long as you keep working you can have the things you need in life. When it comes down to it, we are all on this Earth for a very short time, and I can't understand why people go out of their way to make life miserable for others when there is no good reason for it. A lot of times I did what seemed like the right thing to do. You need to love yourself, you have to have your priorities straight, and you have to give back. In the long run, God will bless you for that.

JAMES M. KILBY

Freedom Fund Award

James was one of the first nineteen black students to integrate an all white high school in Front Royal, Virginia in 1959. He was also one of the first two blacks to formally graduate from Warren County High School in 1961. At 15 years of age, his father enrolled him as a NAACP Youth Member.

Mr. James Menefee Kilby was employed by the Central Intelligence Agency, Washington, DC where his responsibilities included details to the White House. He worked for The White House, as a Senior Messenger serving as Courier to government facilities in the District of Columbia, Virginia and Maryland. He also worked at the Veterans Administration, Washington, DC, as an Administrative Assistant to the Assistant Director of the Benefits Office.

In addition Mr. Kilby's Military served the District of Columbia Army National Guard, Military Police specialized in Field Communications. As a National Guardsman, he was called up for 12 days in 1968 to help quell the riots after the assassination of Martin Luther King, Jr. He was also called out to help with the protection of former President Richard Nixon during the Inaugural Parade from the protestors opposed to the Vietnam War.

On June 21, 1986, James showed his concern against apartheid by sending a letter to then President Pieter W. Botha to the South African Embassy. He was thrilled to receive a detailed response within 15 days from the Secretary of the Embassy. The South African government freed Nelson Mandella in 1990 after 27 years.

Kilby's associations include; Asbury Broadneck United Methodist Church, Usher Board Member,
Founder of T.E.A.R. - Treat Every American Right which was founded in May 1992,
2nd Vice President of the NAACP Board of Directors , Chairman of the NAACP Education Committee,
NAACP Representative on the Committee for Education Equity Community Relations,
Member of the Concerned Black Males Group, Black Military History Institute,
Member of the Black Political Forum of Anne Arundel County Inc.,
American Legion Post 141, Board Member of the Bates Foundation.

1993 - Organized a fund raiser for the African American gentleman who exposed the infamous
        Watergate break in which led to the resignation of President Richard Nixon.
1991 - Recognition, after 30 years, for being one of the first two blacks who formally graduated from
        Warren County High School in 1961.
1991 - Recognition from Governor Schaffer for Volunteerism Certificate for participating in the
        NAACP sponsor SAT/PSAT Institute 1
1990 - Featured in the Capital Newspaper while performing research on the history of a World War I
        poster of Black Soldiers.

James Menefee Kilby a native of Flint Hill Virginia is the proud son of James W. and Catherine Kilby. He is also the father of Racquelia S. Kilby and Jamont V. Kilby, and the grandfather of Trevon J. Kilby-Neal.

Mr. Kilby's spirit of service has enriches the lives of all who meets him.

Anne Arundel County Public Schools
Building Futures . . .

Carol S. Parham, Ed.D., *Acting Superintendent of Schools*

Annapolis Senior High School
2700 Riva Road
Annapolis, Maryland 21401
Telephone: (410) 266-5240

June 30, 1994

Mr. James M. Kilby
2048 Friendly Place
Crofton, MD   21114

Dear Mr. Kilby:

On behalf of the students that you volunteered your services to assist in their academic and social development, I extend to you a special thanks.

I commend you on your dedication and commitment to assist Black male students become responsible student citizens. Through your program, the "Concerned Black Males", I have seen many students become more responsible for their performance and social well-being. The "Making A Leader" component of the program assisted students in developing leadership skills and self-confidence.

Again, many thanks for establishing a positive partnership with the school.

Sincerely yours,

(Mrs.) Laura P. Webb
Principal

LPW:jap

Crusader's group promotes equal treatment for all

By JOETTA SACK
Staff Writer

James Kilby can vividly remember sleeping on the floor of his childhood home in Front Royal, Va. out of fear of being killed.

The Crofton resident and his siblings experienced the effects of racism firsthand when their father pressured the local school board to allow his children to attend the whites-only high school near their home.

In spite of angry neighbors who "shot at the house," Mr. Kilby's father persisted through the state court system, and his children were among the first blacks to attend Warren Co. High School in 1959.

His father's perserverance left an impact on Mr. Kilby, who has since devoted his time to helping other individuals. A member of the NAACP since he was 15-years-old, he has been a long-time crusader for civil rights. His interest is evident on the walls of his Crofton condominium, which are covered with framed newspaper clippings of landmarks in civil rights history, including articles about his family's plight and his hard-earned high school diploma.

As part of his crusade, Mr. Kilby has founded Treat Every American Right, an organization to promote unity and seek justice for individuals treated unfairly.

TEAR honored Frank Wills, the security guard who reported the Watergate burglary, at its first benefit dinner last Wednesday.

"This was my first attempt to help an individual which I feel did not get fair treatment," Mr. Kilby said. "That's what I'm about — to help those who are mistreated."

Mr. Kilby said he had a keen interest in Mr. Wills since the Watergate scandal, when Mr. Kilby was a senior messenger in the White House.

"Mr. Wills has always been in the back of my mind," Mr. Kilby said. After reading a *Jet* magazine article describing Mr. Will's struggle against poverty in March, he decided to contact him at his home in South Carolina.

Mr. Kilby said Mr. Wills deserved

JAMES KILBY
Founder of TEAR

the award because of his heroic efforts during Watergate. Mr. Wills gained notoriety after he discovered tape on the latch of a door at the Watergate complex and called police. The call led to the arrest of burglars hiding inside the Democratic National Committee offices. The scandal eventually led to the resignation of former President Richard Nixon.

"He uncovered the greatest scandal in the history of American politics," Mr. Kilby said. "If anybody deserves it, he does."

Mr. Wills, who said he has worked at a variety of jobs since the Watergate incident, is currently unemployed. He said he spent the past few years taking care of his mother, who died in 1990.

He was also disabled in a car accident several years ago, but said he was denied disability benefits.

"(The benefit) will help him get back on his feet," Mr. Kilby said. "The rest is up to him."

The dinner attracted 125 and raised $750 for Mr. Wills.

"I figure that wasn't too bad," Mr. Kilby said. "I was sweating up until the last minute."

Mr. Wills, who said he was surprised at the honor, was hoping to start his own business with the proceeds of the benefit and make repairs on the home he inherited from his mother.

(See TEAR, Page A13)

TEAR

(Continued from Page A1)

Mr. Kilby recognized the need for TEAR after he wrote a letter to *The Capital* protesting the first Rodney King trial verdict. He formed TEAR in 1992 as a result of the positive response he received to the letter.

The group is made up of seven family members and friends, although it may expand after recent publicity, Mr. Kilby said.

Mr. Kilby is also involved in many other local organizations including serving as second vice president to the board of directors for the county NAACP. He will be honored with a Freedom Award this month.

Mr. Kilby said he has several ideas on who TEAR will honor next but declined to name prospects.

Donations for Mr. Wills may be sent to PO Box 3102, Crofton, MD 21114-0102.

Childhood experience fuels volunteer's goals

By PEGGY RIEMAN
Staff Writer

He recalls a cross burning in his yard when he was a child. He remembers men shooting at his house while he and his family huddled away from the windows.

These are a few of the many profound childhood experiences in Front Royal, Va., that drive James Kilby, *The Capital's* "Volunteer of the Week," to play an influential part in the lives of young black Americans.

Mr. Kilby, 52, is the chairman for the Education Committee of the local chapter of the National Association for the Advancement of Colored People.

Last May he represented the Anne Arundel County NAACP at two high school awards assemblies. He presented Academic Achievement Awards to the outstanding minority senior students who maintained a superior grade point average throughout high school.

He served on the Committee for Education Equity Community Relations, and worked with other groups to

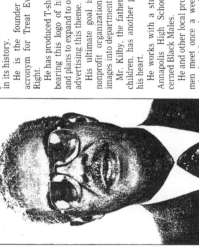

VOLUNTEER OF THE WEEK

James Kilby

reopen Adams Park Elementary School, a school that primarily served children from the black community.

Mr. Kilby has been a member of NAACP since he was 15 years old, and is the current second vice president. Last fall he was chairman of the annual banquet that drew more than 800 people — one of the best attended banquets in its history.

He is the founder of TEAR, an acronym for Treat Every American Right.

He has produced T-shirts and jackets bearing this logo of his organization and plans to expand to offer other items advertising this theme.

His ultimate goal is to set up a nonprofit organization to get these images into department stores.

Mr. Kilby, the father of two grown children, has another project close to his heart.

He works with a student group at Annapolis High School called Concerned Black Males.

He and other local professional black men meet once a week at the high school with student CBM members who have pledged to work with their peers.

The meetings are designed to be nonthreatening, but the goal is to help students find alternative methods to working out problems.

The hope is to show the students that there are concerned and caring adult black males for them to emulate, and peers who are supportive of positive behavior.

Mr. Kilby is in the process of writing a book about his father, a civil rights leader with only a sixth-grade education.

He says his father insisted on quality education for his children.

He put his life on the line in the 1950s for the right to send his children and other black children in Virginia to the same schools as the white children.

As a result of his father's selfless actions, James Kilby was one of the first two black children to graduate from Warren County High School in Front Royal in 1961.

"I want to deliver a great product that my father and my family would be proud of because he has given a lot to me."

He says his 77-year-old father, still living in Front Royal and actively building homes for low-income people, has been a lifelong inspiration for him.

Black's 1959 conviction was bogus

HATTIESBURG, Miss. (AP) — A prosecutor says once-secret records show a black man who tried to enroll at a white college in the 1950s likely was sent to prison wrongly.

A newspaper story Monday about state Sovereignty Commission documents confirms that Clyde Kennard, who died of cancer in 1963, was framed on a charge of illegal possession of whiskey in 1959, Forrest County District Attorney Glenn White said.

Mr. White said he'll examine whether Mr. Kennard's convictions should be overturned. "The documents tend to substantiate what we've uncovered — that he was not guilty of the possession of alcohol," he said.

The now-defunct Sovereignty Commission was a state-funded spy agency created by the 1956 Legislature to thwart integration.

The documents, made public by the Jackson *Clarion-Ledger*, indicated whiskey may have been planted in Mr. Kennard's car in the fall of 1959 to keep him from being the first black at Mississippi Southern College in Hattiesburg, now the University of Southern Mississippi.

The first black student at Southern was enrolled in 1966.

The Sovereignty Commission records show the plot to keep Mr. Kennard out of the school began in 1958 and once included plans to kill him with a car bomb.

"There is no doubt about the suspicion he was framed," said Erle Johnston, director of the Sovereignty Commission in 1963-68.

The 1977 Legislature sealed the commission's documents until 2027, saying the information could damage reputations, but the *Clarion-Ledger* obtained copies of memos and letters on Mr. Kennard.